OCR

LEVEL 3 FREE STANDING MATHEMATICS QUALIFICATION: ADDITIONAL MATHS EXAM PRACTICE

Val Hanrahan
Andrew Ginty

Series editor:
Roger Porkess

HODDER
EDUCATION
AN HACHETTE UK COMPANY

Hachette UK's policy is to use papers that are natural, renewable and recyclable products and made from wood grown in well-managed forests and other controlled sources. The logging and manufacturing processes are expected to conform to the environmental regulations of the country of origin.

Orders: please contact Hachette UK Distribution, Hely Hutchinson Centre, Milton Road Didcot, Oxfordshire, OX11 7HH.
Telephone: +44 (0)1235 827720. Email education@hachette.co.uk
Lines are open from 9 a.m. to 5 p.m., Monday to Friday.
You can also order through our website: www.hoddereducation.co.uk

ISBN: 978 1 5104 4969 5

© Andrew Ginty and Val Hanrahan 2019

First published in 2019 by
Hodder Education,
An Hachette UK Company
Carmelite House
50 Victoria Embankment
London EC4Y 0DZ
www.hoddereducation.co.uk

Impression number 10 9 8 7 6 5 4 3

Year 2023 2022 2021

Cover photo © Rysuku/stock.adobe.com

Typeset in India by Aptara, Inc.

Printed in the UK by CPI Group

A catalogue record for this title is available from the British Library.

www.carbonbalancedprint.com
CBP2250

ii

Contents

**Full worked solutions and mark schemes are available at
www.hoddereducation.co.uk/OCRAddMathsExamPractice**

Introduction

This book has been written to supplement the Additional Mathematics for OCR textbook, but it could also be used to provide additional exercises for anyone studying Mathematics beyond GCSE. There are over 350 questions to support successful preparation for the specification released by OCR for first assessment in 2019.

Grouped according to topic, the chapters follow the content of the OCR Additional Maths textbook.

Each chapter starts with short questions to support retrieval of content and straightforward application of skills learned during the course. The demand gradually builds through each exercise, with the later questions requiring significant mathematical thinking and, often, problem solving strategies. This reflects the range of styles of question that will be found in the exam.

Answers are provided in this book, and full worked solutions and mark allocations to all questions can be found online at

www.hoddereducation.co.uk/OCRAddMathsExamPractice

1 Algebraic manipulation

Exercise 1.1 Simplifying algebraic fractions

1 Simplify the following.

(i) $\dfrac{4x^2y}{3xy^2}$ (ii) $\dfrac{8x^3y^2}{6x^2y^3}$ (iii) $\dfrac{24x^4y^3}{18x^3y^4}$ (iv) $\dfrac{96x^5y^4}{72x^4y^5}$

2 Simplify the following.

(i) $\dfrac{6x+9}{(2x+3)(3x+2)}$ (ii) $\dfrac{2x^2y^3}{8xy^4}$

(iii) $\dfrac{a^2-4}{a^2+4a+4}$ (iv) $\dfrac{p^2-9}{3p+9}$

3 (i) Simplify the following.

(a) $\dfrac{x+2}{x+1}-\dfrac{x+1}{x+2}$ (b) $\dfrac{x+3}{x+2}-\dfrac{x+2}{x+3}$ (c) $\dfrac{x+4}{x+3}-\dfrac{x+3}{x+4}$

(ii) Use the pattern obtained to predict the simplified form of $\dfrac{x+5}{x+4}-\dfrac{x+4}{x+5}$ and use algebra to check your answer.

4 Simplify the following.

(i) $\dfrac{2x}{3y}\times\dfrac{y^3}{5x^2}$ (ii) $\dfrac{x^2+3x+2}{2x-5}\times\dfrac{4x-10}{x^2+7x+10}$

(iii) $\dfrac{3p^2-12}{p^2+4p}\div\dfrac{p^2+5p+6}{p+4}$ (iv) $\dfrac{(2r+3)^2}{6r}\div\dfrac{r^3}{4r+6}$

5 Simplify the following.

(i) $\dfrac{5}{a^2}-\dfrac{2}{a}$ (ii) $\dfrac{4p}{3}+\dfrac{7p}{9}$

(iii) $\dfrac{3a}{2b}-\dfrac{2a}{3b}$ (iv) $\dfrac{4p}{3q}+\dfrac{3p}{4q}$

6 Simplify the following.

(i) $\dfrac{(2x)^3}{x^2}+\dfrac{7x^2}{4}-\dfrac{4x}{3}-\dfrac{3x^2}{2}$ (ii) $\dfrac{a^3}{(2a)^2}+\dfrac{(3a)^2}{2a}-\dfrac{(2a)^2}{3a}-a$

(iii) $x-\dfrac{(2x)^2}{x^3}+3x(-2x)+\dfrac{4}{x}$ (iv) $p^2+\dfrac{2p}{(3p)^2}-\dfrac{4}{p}+9p$

7 Simplify the following.

(i) $\dfrac{5x}{2x^2+x}+\dfrac{4}{2x+1}$ (ii) $\dfrac{4a+2}{6a^2+a-1}-\dfrac{2a+1}{3a^2+5a-2}$

(iii) $\dfrac{2p}{(p+1)(p-1)}-\dfrac{3p}{(p+1)(p-2)}$ (iv) $\dfrac{3r-1}{r^2-4r+3}+\dfrac{2r+1}{r^2-r-6}$

8 Solve the following equations.

(i) $x+\dfrac{2x}{3}=5$ (ii) $\dfrac{4}{p}-\dfrac{2}{3p}=\dfrac{2}{3}$

(iii) $\dfrac{3}{x^2}=\dfrac{10}{x}-3$ (iv) $\dfrac{4}{x^2}+\dfrac{3}{x}=1$

9 The denominator of a fraction is x.
The numerator is 5 less than the denominator.

If the numerator and denominator are both increased by 3, the value of the new fraction is $\frac{2}{3}$.

Write down an equation for x and solve it.

10 In this question $x \neq \pm 1$. One of the statements below is true for all the allowed values of x, another is true for just one value of x and the remaining one is false for all the allowed values of x. Identify which is which and solve the equation where this is possible.

(i) $\dfrac{x+3}{x-1} - \dfrac{x+2}{x+1} = \dfrac{x+9}{x^2-1}$

(ii) $\dfrac{x+3}{x-1} - \dfrac{x+2}{x+1} = \dfrac{3x+5}{x^2-1}$

(iii) $\dfrac{x+3}{x-1} - \dfrac{x+5}{x+1} = \dfrac{2}{x^2-1}$

Exercise 1.2 Simplifying expressions containing square roots

1 Simplify the following as much as possible.

(i) $\sqrt{2} \times \sqrt{3}$ (ii) $\sqrt{3} \times \sqrt{4}$ (iii) $\sqrt{4} \times \sqrt{5}$

(iv) $\sqrt{2} \times \sqrt{4}$ (v) $\sqrt{4} \times \sqrt{6}$ (vi) $\sqrt{6} \times \sqrt{8}$

2 Simplify the following as much as possible.

(i) $\sqrt{12}$ (ii) $\sqrt{45}$ (iii) $\sqrt{80}$ (iv) $\sqrt{150}$

3 Simplify the following as much as possible.

(i) $\sqrt{54}$ (ii) $\sqrt{8} \times \sqrt{2}$

(iii) $\sqrt{3}(3\sqrt{3} - 2)$ (iv) $\sqrt{8} + \sqrt{18} - 4\sqrt{2}$

4 Write the following as surds in their simplest form.

(i) $\left(2 + \sqrt{3}\right)\left(3 + \sqrt{2}\right)$ (ii) $\left(2 - \sqrt{3}\right)\left(3 + \sqrt{2}\right)$

(iii) $\left(2 + \sqrt{3}\right)\left(3 - \sqrt{2}\right)$ (iv) $\left(2 - \sqrt{3}\right)\left(3 - \sqrt{2}\right)$

5 Write the following as surds in their simplest form.

(i) $(\sqrt{5} + 6)(3 - \sqrt{5})$ (ii) $(3 + 2\sqrt{2})(2 - \sqrt{2})$

(iii) $(7 - \sqrt{3})^2$

6 Simplify the following by rationalising the denominators.

(i) $\dfrac{4}{\sqrt{2}}$ (ii) $\dfrac{\sqrt{27}}{\sqrt{6}}$ (iii) $\dfrac{1}{2\sqrt{2}}$ (iv) $\dfrac{5}{\sqrt{75}}$ (v) $\dfrac{5\sqrt{2}}{2\sqrt{5}}$

7 Write each of the following in its simplest form.

(i) $\sqrt{x^5}$ (ii) $\sqrt{8x^3}$

(iii) $\sqrt{27x}$ (iv) $\sqrt{x^2 y^3} + \sqrt{x^3 y^2}$

(v) $\sqrt{3x^6} + \sqrt{27x^6}$

8 Express each of the following as the square root of a single number.

   (i) $2\sqrt{5}$ **(ii)** $4\sqrt{8}$ **(iii)** $10\sqrt{6}$ **(iv)** $6\sqrt{12}$

9 Simplify the following fractions so that if the answer is a fraction its denominator is a whole number, leaving any square roots in the numerator.

   (i) $\sqrt{\dfrac{16}{49}}$ **(ii)** $\sqrt{\dfrac{125}{3}}$ **(iii)** $\sqrt{\dfrac{8}{27}}$ **(iv)** $\sqrt{\dfrac{18}{75}}$

10 Simplify the following, leaving any square roots in the numerator.

   (i) $\sqrt{\dfrac{x^3}{y^4}}$ **(ii)** $\sqrt{\dfrac{36x^3}{y^2}}$ **(iii)** $\sqrt{\dfrac{x^3}{24y^2}}$ **(iv)** $\sqrt{\dfrac{6xy^5}{42x^2y^3}}$

11 Simplify the following by collecting like terms.

   (i) $\left(2 + \sqrt{3}\right) + \left(3 - 2\sqrt{3}\right)$ **(ii)** $3\left(\sqrt{5} - 1\right) - 2\left(\sqrt{5} + 1\right)$

12 Expand and simplify.

   (i) $\left(\sqrt{12} + 3\right)\left(\sqrt{12} - 3\right)$ **(ii)** $\sqrt{6}\left(9 - 5\sqrt{6}\right)$

   (iii) $\left(5 + 2\sqrt{3}\right)^2$ **(iv)** $\left(3\sqrt{3} - 2\sqrt{2}\right)^2$

13 Expand and simplify.

   (i) $\left(x + 3\sqrt{y}\right)\left(x - 3\sqrt{y}\right)$ **(ii)** $\left(3\sqrt{x} - 5\sqrt{y}\right)^2$

   (iii) $\left(3\sqrt{x} + 5\sqrt{y}\right)^2$ **(iv)** $\sqrt{x^3y}\left(\sqrt{x} - \sqrt{y}\right)$

14 Solve the following equations, giving your answers as simply as possible in exact form.

   (i) $x^2 + 6x - 3 = 0$ **(ii)** $9x^2 - 6x + 1 = 0$

   (iii) $3x^2 - 3x - 1 = 0$

15 Rationalise the denominators, giving each answer in its simplest form.

   (i) $\dfrac{20}{\sqrt{5}}$ **(ii)** $\dfrac{9}{\left(\sqrt{5} - \sqrt{2}\right)}$ **(iii)** $\dfrac{5 - \sqrt{3}}{5 + \sqrt{3}}$

16 Rationalise the denominators, giving each answer in its simplest form.

   (i) $\dfrac{\sqrt{x^3}}{\sqrt{x^2y}}$ **(ii)** $\dfrac{\sqrt{x} + 2\sqrt{y}}{\sqrt{x} - 2\sqrt{y}}$ **(iii)** $\dfrac{2\sqrt{x} + 3\sqrt{y}}{2\sqrt{x} - 3\sqrt{y}}$

17 A right-angled triangle has one side of length $\sqrt{15}$ cm and the hypotenuse is of length $\sqrt{35}$ cm. Find the length of the other side in its simplest surd form.

18 A rectangle has long sides that are double the length of the short sides. Find the area of the rectangle when the diagonal is 12 cm long.

19 The diagram shows a pyramid with a square base of side x cm. The height of the pyramid is twice the length of the base.

   (i) Find an expression for the length of a sloping edge.

   (ii) Given that a sloping edge is $20\sqrt{162}$ cm, find the height of the pyramid.

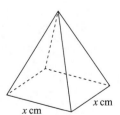

x cm x cm

2 Polynomials, functions and equations

Exercise 2.1 Operations with polynomials

1 State the order of the following polynomials.

  (i) $5x^3 - 2x + 7$ (ii) $6 - 4x^5 + x^2$ (iii) $(2x - 3)^2$

2 (i) Add $(6x^3 + 3x^2 - 2x - 7)$ to $(4x^2 - x - 9)$.

  (ii) Add $(2x^3 - 3x^2 + 4)$ to $(x^3 - 2x + 3)$.

3 (i) Subtract $(x^3 - 3x^2 + 4)$ from $(2x^3 + 3x - 4)$.

  (ii) Subtract $(3x^3 - 2x + 3)$ from $(x^4 + 2x^3 - x^2 + 1)$.

4 (i) Add $(x^3 - 2x^2 - 4x + 7)$ to $(x^3 - 1)$.

  (ii) Add $(2x^3 + 4x^2 - 8x + 14)$ to your answer to part (i).

  (iii) Subtract $(3x^3 + 6x^2 - 12x + 21)$ from your answer to (ii).

  (iv) What do you notice?

5 (i) Add $(2 + 3x - x^3)$ to $(2x^3 - 3x + 2)$.

  (ii) Subtract $(x^2 + 2x - 4)$ from your answer to part (i).

  (iii) Add $(x^3 + x^2 - x - 6)$ to your answer to part (ii).

  (iv) What do you notice?

6 (i) Multiply $(2x^2 - 3x - 2)$ by $(3x - 1)$.

  (ii) Multiply $(2x^4 - 3)$ by $(3x^2 + 5x + 1)$.

7 (i) Multiply $(3x - 1)^2$ by $(2x^3 - 3)$.

  (ii) Multiply $(x - 2)^2$ by $(x + 2)^2$.

8 (i) Divide $(x^3 + 2x^2 - x - 2)$ by $(x - 1)$.

  (ii) Divide $(2x^3 - 7x^2 + 7x - 2)$ by $(2x - 1)$.

9 (i) Divide $(x^4 + 4x^2 - 5)$ by $(x^2 - 1)$.

  (ii) Divide $(2x^3 + x + 18)$ by $(x + 2)$.

10 (i) Multiply $(x + 2)^2$ by $(x - 4)^2$.

  (ii) Divide your answer to part (i) by $(x^2 - 2x - 8)$.

  (iii) What do you notice?

11 (i) Simplify $(2x^3 + 3x^2 - 5) - (3x - 2)^2$.

  (ii) Simplify $(x + 1)(x^2 - 1) - (x - 1)(x^2 + 1)$.

12 (i) Simplify $(x - 1)^2(4x + 1) - (3x - 1)(x + 1)^2$.

  (ii) Simplify $(5x^3 - 2x + 3) - (2x - 5)^2$.

Exercise 2.2 The factor theorem, completing the square and the quadratic formula

1 **(i)** Show that $x^3 - 2x^2 - 5x + 6$ is divisible by $(x-1)$.

  (ii) Write $x^3 - 2x^2 - 5x + 6$ in the form $(x-1)(x^2 + ax + b)$ where a and b are to be determined.

  (iii) Hence factorise $x^3 - 2x^2 - 5x + 6$ completely.

2 For each of the following expressions write down the factors of the constant term and then use the factor theorem to factorise it.

  (i) $x^3 - 3x^2 - 6x - 8$

  (ii) $x^3 + 3x^2 + x + 3$

  (iii) $2x^3 + 11x^2 + 17x + 6$

3 **(i)** Divide $2x^3 + 13x^2 + 22x + 3$ by $(x+3)$.

  (ii) Hence show that $2x^3 + 13x^2 + 22x + 3 = 0$ has only one integer root.

4 Find the possible values of a if $(x-2)$ is a factor of $x^3 + x^2 - 5ax + 2a^2$.

5 The polynomial $\mathrm{f}(x) = x^3 + ax^2 + bx - 8$ has factors $(x-1)$ and $(x+2)$. Find the values of a and b and the other linear factor.

6 Show that $x = 3$ is a root of the equation $2x^3 - 3x^2 - 11x + 6 = 0$ and hence solve the equation completely.

7 **(i)** Which of the following three expressions have $(x+2)$ as a factor?

  (a) $x^3 - x^2 - 10x - 12$

  (b) $x^3 + x^2 - 8x - 12$

  (c) $2x^3 - x^2 - 10x + 4$

  (ii) Add the three polynomials in part **(i)** together.

  (iii) Divide the answer to part **(ii)** by $(x+2)$.

  (iv) What do you notice?

8 Use the method of completing the square to solve the following equations, leaving square roots in your answers.

  (i) $x^2 - 6x + 2 = 0$

  (ii) $x^2 - 6x - 2 = 0$

  (iii) $x^2 + 6x + 2 = 0$

  (iv) $x^2 + 6x - 2 = 0$

9 Solve the following equations.

  (i) $x^2 - 4x + 3 = 0$

  (ii) $x^2 - 4x - 3 = 0$

  (iii) $x^2 + 4x + 3 = 0$

  (iv) $x^2 + 4x - 3 = 0$

10 The diagram shows sketches of the graphs of $y = f(x)$ and $y = g(x)$ where

$f(x) = x^3 + x^2 - 5x + 3$ and $g(x) = \dfrac{(x+3)^2}{3}$.

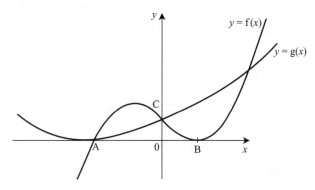

(i) Use the factor theorem to factorise $f(x)$.

(ii) Find the coordinates of the points A, B and C.

(iii) Find the coordinates of the other point of intersection of the two curves.

11 (i) Determine whether each of the following is a factor of the expression $x^3 - 19x + 30$. You must show your working.

(a) $(x - 2)$

(b) $(x - 3)$

(ii) Factorise the expression $x^3 - 19x + 30$.

(iii) Solve the equation $x^3 - 19x + 30 = 0$.

12 The diagram shows an open rectangular tank with a square base of side x metres and a volume of $18\,\text{m}^3$.

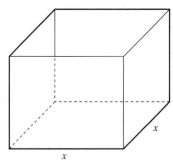

(i) Write down an expression in terms of x for the height of the tank.

(ii) Show that the surface area of the tank is $\left(x^2 + \dfrac{72}{x}\right)\text{m}^2$.

(iii) Given that the surface area is $33\,\text{m}^2$, show that $x^3 - 33x + 72 = 0$.

(iv) Use the factor theorem to find a factor of $x^3 - 33x + 72 = 0$.

(v) Solve $x^3 - 33x + 72 = 0$ and hence find possible dimensions for the tank.

13 The height of a ball, $h\,\text{m}$, at a time t seconds is given by $h = 1.5 + 20t - 5t^2$. Show that the ball does not reach a height of 25 metres.

14 Find (to 2 d.p.) the coordinates of the points of intersection of the line
$y = 2x + 1$ and the circle $x^2 + y^2 = 25$.

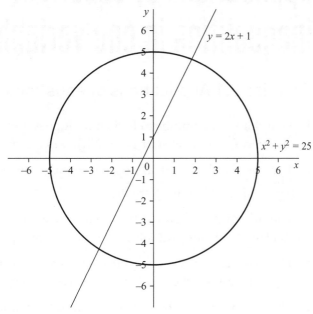

3

Applications of equations and inequalities in one variable

Exercise 3.1 Applications of equations

1 Sean thinks of a number. He then multiplies it by 5, adds 2, divides the result by 4 and the answer is 13. What was the number?

2 The two equal sides of an isosceles triangle have lengths $(x + 2)$ cm and $\left(\dfrac{3x}{4} + 4\right)$ cm. How long are they?

3 The sum of the squares of two consecutive integers is 113. Form a quadratic equation and solve it to find the two possible pairs of integers.

4 The diameters of two concentric circles are $(x + 4)$ cm and $(x + 6)$ cm and the area between them is $10\pi\,\text{cm}^2$. What are their radii?

5 The area of a square of side $(x + 2)$ cm is four times the area of a square of side x cm. Form an equation in x and solve it to find the dimensions of the two squares.

6 Ross throws a ball horizontally from a height of 1.6 metres above the side of a hill so that its trajectory follows the line of greatest slope.

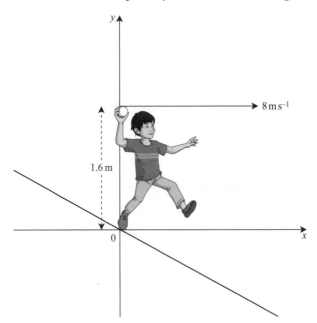

Taking the origin as the point where Ross is standing, and the initial speed of the ball as $8\,\text{m}\,\text{s}^{-1}$ the path of the ball is given by the pair of simultaneous equations $x = 8t$ and $y = 1.6 - 5t^2$, where t is the time in seconds.
The equation of the side of the hill is given by $y = -0.5x$.

Find the value of t when the ball first bounces off the hillside.

7 A tube of sweets has a circular cross-section of diameter 6 cm and a volume of 500 cm³.

(i) What is the height of the tube to the nearest millimetre?

The top and the base are made of metal and the wall of the tube is made of cardboard.

(ii) What are the dimensions of the piece of cardboard to the nearest millimetre?

8 A cat is sitting on the garden wall when it sees a mouse 2 m away horizontally. The wall is 1.25 m high and the cat jumps horizontally from the wall with speed u m s⁻¹ and lands on the mouse.

The position of the cat at time t seconds is given in metres by coordinates (x, y) relative to an origin at the base of the wall.

The horizontal acceleration of the cat is zero and the vertical acceleration is 10 m s⁻² downwards.

Using $s = ut + \dfrac{1}{2}at^2$ find the initial speed of the cat.

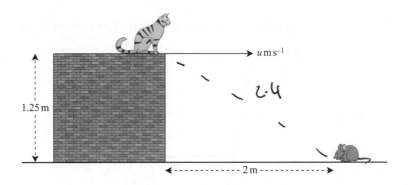

Exercise 3.2 Linear and quadratic inequalities and their illustrations

1 Solve each of the following inequalities and illustrate the solution on a number line.

(i) $4(x - 1) > 3(x - 2)$ **(ii)** $4(x - 1) \geqslant 3(x - 2)$

(iii) $4(x - 1) < 3(x - 2)$ **(iv)** $4(x - 1) \leqslant 3(x - 2)$

2 Solve each of the following inequalities and illustrate the solution on a number line.

(i) $(x + 3)(x - 4) < 0$ **(ii)** $(x + 3)(x - 4) \leqslant 0$

(iii) $(x + 3)(x - 4) > 0$ **(iv)** $(x + 3)(x - 4) \geqslant 0$

3 Express each of the line segments drawn in bold type in algebraic form.

(i)

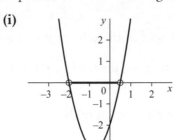

(ii)

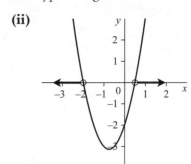

(iii)

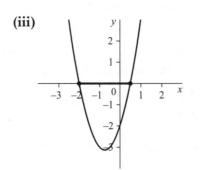

(iv)

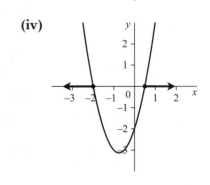

4 Find the solution sets identified in each of the following graphs.

(i)

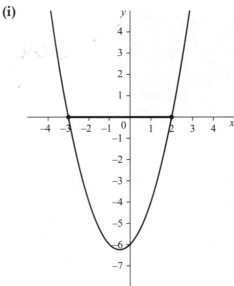

(ii)

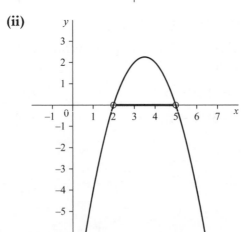

(iii)

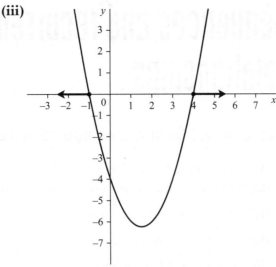

(iv)

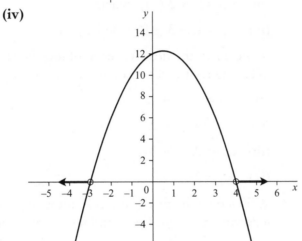

5 The area of a square of side x cm is greater than the area of a rectangle with sides $(x - 1)$ cm and $(x + 2)$ cm. Find the range of possible values of x.

6 Two positive whole numbers differ by five and their product is less than fifty. Find the range of possible values for the smaller number.

7 Draw separate diagrams illustrating each of the following inequalities.

(i) $-2 < x < 3$

(ii) $x < -2$ or $x > 3$

(iii) $x \leqslant -2$ or $x \geqslant 3$

(iv) $-2 \leqslant x \leqslant 3$

8 (i) The perimeter of a rectangle, with sides $(2x + 1)$ cm and x cm, is greater than that of a square with sides $(x + 1)$ cm. What can you say about x?

(ii) What would be the value of x if the two shapes had equal areas? Give your answer in exact form as a surd.

9 (i) Solve the equation $x^2 - 6x - 7 = 0$.

(ii) Sketch the graph of $y = x^2 - 6x - 7$.

(iii) Solve the inequality $x^2 - 6x - 7 \leqslant 0$.

(iv) Illustrate your answer to part **(iii)** on a copy of your sketch graph.

10 (i) Solve the equation $3 + 2x - 3x^2 = 0$ giving your answers to 2 decimal places.

(ii) Sketch the graph of $y = 3 + 2x - 3x^2$.

(iii) Solve the inequality $3 + 2x - 3x^2 > 0$.

(iv) Illustrate your answer to part **(iii)** on a copy of your sketch graph.

4 Sequences and recurrence relationships

Exercise 4.1 Sequences and recurrence relationships

1 Write down the first four terms of the sequences generated by the following recurrence relationships and say what you notice.

   (i) $x_{n+1} = x_n + 3$ where $x_1 = 0$

   (ii) $x_{n+1} = x_n - 3$ where $x_1 = 0$

   (iii) $x_{n+1} = x_n + 3\,(-1)^n$ where $x_1 = 0$

   (iv) $x_{n+1} = x_n - 3\,(-1)^n$ where $x_1 = 0$

2 Write down the first five terms of the sequences generated by the following recurrence relationships. In each case $x_1 = 2$ and $x_2 = -2$.

   (i) $x_{n+2} = 3x_{n+1} - 2x_n$

   (ii) $x_{n+2} = 3x_{n+1} + 2x_n$

   (iii) $x_{n+2} = 2x_{n+1} - 3x_n$

   (iv) $x_{n+2} = 2x_{n+1} + 3x_n$

3 Write down the first four terms of the sequences generated by the following recurrence relationships. In each case $x_1 = 6$.

   (i) $x_{n+1} = x_n + 3(-2)^n$

   (ii) $x_{n+1} = x_n - 3(-2)^n$

   (iii) $x_{n+1} = x_n + 2(-3)^n$

   (iv) $x_{n+1} = x_n - 2(-3)^n$

4 Find the first four terms of the sequence defined by $x_{n+1} = 3x_n - 2$ when

   (i) $x_1 = 1$ **(ii)** $x_1 = -1$ **(iii)** $x_1 = 0$.

5 A sequence is defined by the relationship $u_n = 2^n - 3n + 1$.
   Find the first, fifth and tenth terms.

6 The first two terms of a sequence of the form $u_n = a^n - b^n + 4$ are 5 and 9.

   (i)   Find the values of a and b.

   (ii) Show that $u_3 = 23$.

   (iii) Find the value of the sixth term.

7 Sequence A is defined by $u_n = 2n - 2$.
   Sequence B is defined by $u_{n+1} = u_n + 2$, $u_1 = 0$.

   (i)   Write down the first four terms of sequence A.

   (ii) Write down the first four terms of sequence B.

   (iii) What do you notice?

   (iv) Use algebra to prove that your answer for part **(iii)** is true for all values of n.

8 The terms of a sequence are defined by $u_n = 3 + (-1)^n \times 2$.

    (i) Write down the first five terms of this sequence.

    (ii) Describe what happens to the terms of this sequence as n increases if it is changed to

        (a) $u_n = 3 + (-2)^n \times 2$ **(b)** $u_n = 3 + \left(-\dfrac{1}{2}\right)^n \times 2$.

9 **(i)** Show that the equation $x^2 - 5x - 1 = 0$ can be rearranged to give $x = \pm\sqrt{5x + 1}$.

    (ii) Taking $x_1 = 1$, calculate $x_2 = \sqrt{5x_1 + 1}$.

    (iii) State the recurrence relationship that this will generate.

    (iv) Use this relationship to find a root of the equation $x^2 - 5x - 1 = 0$.

10 **(i)** Show that the equation $x^3 + 3x - 1 = 0$ can be rearranged to give $x = \dfrac{1 - x^3}{3}$.

    (ii) Starting with $x_1 = 0$, use your calculator to find the sequence generated by the recurrence relation $x_{n+1} = \dfrac{1 - x_n^3}{3}$, continuing until your answer to 4 s.f. does not change.

    (iii) Check that this value is an approximation for a root of the original equation.

    (iv) What happens if you try to use the rearrangement $x = \sqrt[3]{1 - 3x}$?

11 The cost, £v_1, of a house when it was bought on 1 January 2001 was £250 000. On 1 January 2002 its value was £v_2 and so on.

    It is observed that $v_{n+1} = 1.04v_n$.

    (i) Write down the annual percentage increase in the value of the house.

    (ii) How much will it be worth after seven years?

    (iii) How long will it take before it is worth at least £500 000 assuming that this rate continues?

12 The cost, £p_1, of a new caravan when it was bought on 1 June 2011 was £24 000.

    One year later, on 1 June 2012, its market value was £p_2 and so on.

    The caravan depreciated at a rate of 10% per annum.

    (i) Write down a recurrence relation connecting p_{n+1} and p_n.

    (ii) Find the market value of the caravan after

        (a) 2 years   **(b)** 5 years.

    (iii) If instead depreciation is calculated at a rate of 5% every 6 months, find new estimates for the market value of the caravan after

        (a) 2 years   **(b)** 5 years.

5 Points, lines and circles

Exercise 5.1 Points and lines

1 A is the point $(-1,3)$ and B is the point $(5,11)$. Calculate

   (i) the gradient of the line AB

   (ii) the gradient of the line perpendicular to AB

   (iii) the length of AB

   (iv) the coordinates of the midpoint of AB.

2 The points O, P and Q are $(0,0)$, $(3,4)$ and $(9,12)$ respectively.

   (i) Find the distance between

   (a) O and P   (b) P and Q   (c) O and Q.

   (ii) Find the gradient of

   (a) OP   (b) PQ   (c) OQ.

   (iii) What do your answers to parts (i) and (ii) tell you about the points O, P and Q?

3 (i) Show that the points $A(-2,3)$, $B(1,5)$ and $C(7,9)$ are collinear and find the equation of the line.

   (ii) How far is B from the midpoint of AC?

4 The line $y = 2x + c$ passes through the midpoint of the line AB with $A(1,2)$ and $B(7,8)$. Find the value of c.

5 The points A, B, and C have coordinates $(-1,4)$, $(2,8)$ and $(6,5)$ respectively. Show that the triangle ABC is isosceles.

6 Given that A and B are the points $(1,2)$ and $(5,2)$ respectively, find the coordinates of the point C so that triangle ABC is equilateral. Give your answer in surd form. (There are two possible answers.)

7 The points $A(1,-3)$, $B(6,2)$, $C(8,5)$ and D are the vertices of a parallelogram. Find the coordinates of D.

8 (i) Find the coordinates of the points where each of the following lines intersect the coordinate axes.

   (a) $3x - y = 6$ (b) $x - 5y + 5 = 0$ (c) $2x + 3y = 4$

   (ii) Which line segment between the axes is the shortest?

   (iii) Draw all three lines on the same graph.

9 Sketch the following pairs of lines on the same axes and solve their equations simultaneously to find their point of intersection.

   (i) $y = 3x - 2$ (ii) $2x + 3y = 12$ (iii) $3x + y = 4$
   $x + y = 2$ $x - 2y = -1$ $5x - 2y = 3$

10 When the market price £p of an article sold on the free market varies, so does the number demanded D and the number supplied S. In one case $D = 20 + 0.1p$ and $S = p - 16$.

   (i) Sketch both of these lines on the same graph. (Put p on the horizontal axis.)

The market reaches a state of equilibrium when the number demanded equals the number supplied.

(ii) Find the equilibrium price and the number bought and sold when the market is in equilibrium.

11 The line with equation $4x + 2y = 20$ meets the x-axis at A and the line $y = x + 4$ meets the y-axis at B. The two lines intersect at the point C.

(i) Sketch the two lines on the same diagram.

(ii) Calculate the coordinates of the points A, B and C.

(iii) Calculate the area of triangle OBC where O is the origin.

(iv) Find the coordinates of the point D such that ABCD is a parallelogram.

Exercise 5.2 Circles

1 Find the equations of the following circles.

(i) centre $(1,1)$, radius 2

(ii) centre $(2,5)$, radius 3

(iii) centre $(-1,-4)$, radius 5

2 For the circle $(x + 1)^2 + (y - 2)^2 = 4$

(i) state the radius and the coordinates of the centre of the circle

(ii) plot the circle.

(iii) Does the point $(0,1.75)$ lie inside the circle, on the circle or outside the circle?

3 Calculate the equation of the circle in each diagram.

(i)

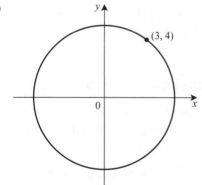

(ii)

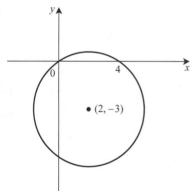

(iii)

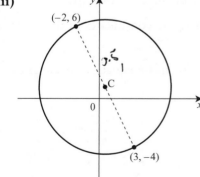

4 Show that the equation $x^2 + y^2 + 4x - 2y + 1 = 0$ represents a circle. Hence state the radius of the circle, give the coordinates of the centre and draw the circle.

5 Determine whether the origin lies inside or outside the circle with equation $x^2 + y^2 - 6x + 8y = 11$.

6 Determine where the circles with the following equations touch either of the coordinate axes. In each case say which axis (or both) and give the coordinates of the point of contact.

   (i) $(x - 3)^2 + (y - 2)^2 = 4$

   (ii) $(x - 1)^2 + (y + 1)^2 = 1$

   (iii) $(x - 5)^2 + (y - 5)^2 = 25$

   (iv) $(x + 1)^2 + (y + 2)^2 = 1$

7 Both of the following pairs of equations give a line and a circle. In each case, determine whether the line intersects the circle, is a tangent to it or fails to meet it. You do not need to find the coordinates of any points of intersection.

   (i) $x + y = 8$ **(ii)** $2x + y = 5$

       $x^2 + y^2 = 25$ $(x - 4)^2 + (y - 2)^2 = 5$

8 Show that the line with equation $4x + 3y = 12$ does not intersect the circle $x^2 + y^2 = 4$.

9 **(i)** Draw the circles $(x + 1)^2 + (y - 4)^2 = 16$ and $(x - 5)^2 + (y - 4)^2 = 16$ on the same axes.

   (ii) Use algebra to find their points of intersection.

   (iii) Find the equation of the line joining their centres and the equation of the line joining their points of intersection. What is the angle between these two lines?

10 **(i)** Draw the circles $(x - 1)^2 + (y - 2)^2 = 1$ and $(x - 2)^2 + (y - 1)^2 = 1$ on the same axes.

   (ii) Use algebra to find their points of intersection.

   (iii) Find the equation of the line joining their centres and the equation of the line joining their points of intersection. What is the angle between these two lines?

11 A circle passes through the points A(2,3), B(6,5) and C(3,11).

   (i) Calculate the lengths of the sides of triangle ABC and hence show that AC is a diameter of the circle.

   (ii) Calculate the coordinates of the centre of the circle and the radius of the circle.

   (iii) Write down the equation of the circle.

6 Graphs

Exercise 6.1 Cartesian graphs

1   Sketch each set of three lines on the same graph, marking the points of intersection with the axes.

    (i) **(a)** $y = x - 2$ **(b)** $y = x - 3$ **(c)** $y = x - 4$

    (ii) **(a)** $y = x + 1$ **(b)** $y = 2x + 1$ **(c)** $y = 3x + 1$

    (iii) **(a)** $y = x - 1$ **(b)** $y = 2x - 2$ **(c)** $y = 3x - 3$

2   **(i)** Sketch the following four lines on the same axes.

        (a) $3x - 2y = 6$ **(b)** $3x - 2y = -6$

        (c) $3x + 2y = 6$ **(d)** $3x + 2y = -6$

    (ii) State the precise sort of parallelogram that is formed by the lines.

3   Factorise the following equations and hence sketch the curves, marking the points of intersection with the axes.

    (i) $y = x^2 - x - 6$

    (ii) $y = 2x^2 - 3x - 2$

    (iii) $y = 3x^2 + 7x - 6$

4   **(i)** Plot the curve $y = x^3 - 3x + 4$ for $-3 \leqslant x \leqslant 3$.

    (ii) On the same axes draw the curve $y = x^2 - 3x + 4$.

    (iii) From your graph, state the coordinates of the points of intersection of the two graphs.

    (iv) Confirm your answer algebraically.

5   **(i)** Plot the curve $y = 6 - 4x^2 - x^3$ for $-4 \leqslant x \leqslant 2$.

    (ii) From your graph, state the coordinates of the points of intersection with the line $y = 6$.

    (iii) Confirm your answer algebraically.

6   **(i)** Plot the curve $y = (x - 2)^2 (x + 2)^2$ for $-3 \leqslant x \leqslant 3$.

    (ii) From your graph state any symmetries of the curve.

    (iii) Add the graph of $y = -(x - 2)^2 (x + 2)^2$ to your graph.

    (iv) State any symmetries of the two combined graphs.

7   **(i)** Plot the curve $y = x^4 + 4x^3 - 4x - 5$ for $-4 \leqslant x \leqslant 2$.

    (ii) Calculate the coordinates of any points of intersection of this curve and the curve $y = x^4 - 5$.

8   **(i)** Plot the curve $y = x^3 - 3x + 4$ for $-3 \leqslant x \leqslant 3$.

    (ii) Find the exact coordinates of the points where the curve crosses the line $y = 4$.

    (iii) What can you say about the symmetry of the curve $y = x^3 - 3x + 4$?

9 Find the equations of the four sides of the diamond shape below.

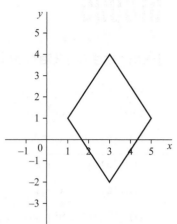

10 Use these graphs to find the equations of their curves.

(i)

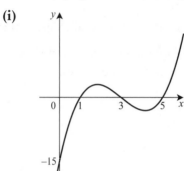

(ii)

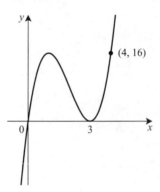

(iii)

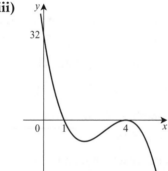

(iv)

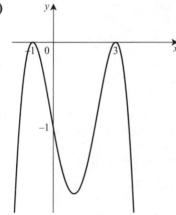

Exercise 6.2 Trigonometric and exponential graphs

1 **(i)** Plot the graphs of $y = \sin x$ and $y = \sin(x - 60°)$ on the same axes for $0° \leqslant x \leqslant 180°$.

 (ii) What do you notice about these graphs?

 (iii) Without drawing up a table, sketch the graph of $y = \sin(x - 30°)$ for $0° \leqslant x \leqslant 180°$, marking the coordinates of the points of intersection with the axes.

2 **(i)** Draw the graph of $y = \sin^2 x - \sin x$ for $0° \leqslant x \leqslant 360°$.

 (ii) From the graph, state values of x in the interval $0° \leqslant x \leqslant 360°$ for which $\sin^2 x - \sin x = 0$.

 (iii) Explain how you could answer part **(ii)** without using the graph.

3 **(i)** Plot the graphs of $y = \tan x$, $y = -\tan x$ and $y = \tan(-x)$ on the same axes for $0° \leqslant x \leqslant 60°$.

 (ii) List any symmetries that you can see.

4 **(i)** Plot the graphs of $y = \cos x$ and $y = \cos x + 1$ on the same axes for $0° \leqslant x \leqslant 180°$.

 (ii) What do you notice about these graphs?

5 **(i)** Plot the graph of $y = \sin x - \cos x$ for $0° \leqslant x \leqslant 360°$.

 (ii) On the same axes sketch the graph of $y = \cos x - \sin x$ for $0° \leqslant x \leqslant 360°$.

 (iii) State the connection between the graphs that allowed you to sketch the second one.

6 The graph below shows the curves $y = x^2$ and $y = 2^x$.

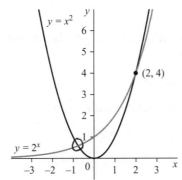

 (i) The two curves intersect at the point $(2, 4)$. Use trial and improvement to find the other point of intersection to 3 d.p.

 (ii) (a) Copy the graph of the two curves and add the graph of $y = 2^{-x}$ to your copy.

   (b) State the coordinates of the points of intersection of the graphs $y = x^2$ and $y = 2^{-x}$.

7 Match the correct equation to each of the graphs.

(i) $y = 2^x + 1$ **(ii)** $y = 2^{-x} + 1$

(iii) $y = 2^{x+1}$ **(iv)** $y = 2^{-x+1}$

(a)

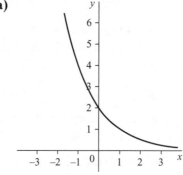

(b)

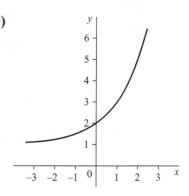

(c)

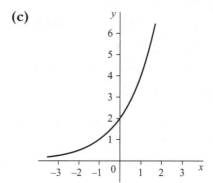

(d)

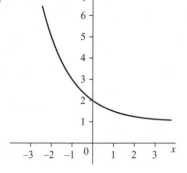

8 (i) Use your knowledge of graphs to sketch $y = x^3$ and $y = 3^x$ on the same axes.

   (ii) List any similarities and differences between the two graphs.

9 (i) Describe the relationship between the following pairs of graphs.

     (a) $y = 2^x$ and $y = 2^{-x}$

     (b) $y = 3 + 2^x$ and $y = 3 - 2^x$

     (c) $y = 3 + 2^{-x}$ and $y = 3 - 2^{-x}$

   (ii) Use your conclusions in part **(i)** to sketch all four curves in **(b)** and **(c)** on the same axes.

10 (i) On the same axes plot the graphs of $y = 2^x$ and $y = 3^x$ for $-2 \leqslant x \leqslant 1$.

   (ii) Add the graph of $y = 3^x - 2^x$.

   (iii) Describe what happens in part **(ii)** for negative values of x and when $x \to -\infty$.

Linear inequalities in two variables

Exercise 7.1 Graphing inequalities

1

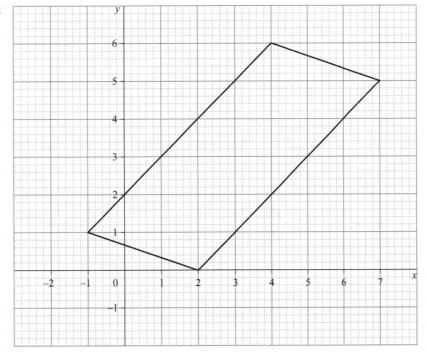

(i) Write down the equations of the four lines which define the rectangle above.

(ii) Write down the four inequalities that define the rectangle.

(iii) Which of the following points are in the feasible region?

   (a) $(1,2)$ **(b)** $(0,5)$ **(c)** $(2,-2)$

2

(i) Write down the equations of the four sides of the parallelogram above.

(ii) Write down the four inequalities that define the parallelogram.

(iii) Which of the following points are in the feasible region?

   (a) $(3,2)$ **(b)** $(2,5)$ **(c)** $(6,3)$

3 (i) On a single diagram illustrate the region defined by all of the following inequalities.

    (a) $x + y \geqslant 1$ **(b)** $x + y \leqslant 3$

    (c) $y \geqslant x - 1$ **(d)** $y \leqslant x + 1$

(ii) State, as fully as possible, the shape of the region defined by the four inequalities.

(iii) Is the point $(1.5, 1.4)$ in the feasible region?

4 (i) On a single diagram illustrate the region defined by all of the following inequalities.

    (a) $x > 2$ **(b)** $y \geqslant 0$

    (c) $y \leqslant x$ **(d)** $2x + 3y < 12$

(ii) Is the point $(2, 1)$ in the feasible region?

5

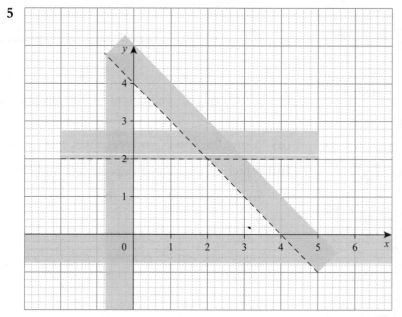

(i) Write down the inequalities that define the region illustrated.

(ii) How many points in this region have integer coefficients?

6 On separate 2-dimensional diagrams use shading to denote each of these inequalities.

    (i) $-2 < x < 4$ **(ii)** $3 \leqslant y < 6$

    (iii) $2 \leqslant x + 3y \leqslant 6$ **(iv)** $7 > x - 2y \geqslant 4$

7 (i) On the same axes, illustrate the regions defined by these inequalities.
$$x > 2 \qquad 2x + 3y \leqslant 12 \qquad y > -2$$

(ii) Are the following points in the region defined by all three inequalities?

    (a) $(3, -1)$ **(b)** $(4, 2)$ **(c)** $(2, 1)$

8 (i) On the same axes illustrate the region defined by these inequalities.
$$x < 5 \qquad y < x + 2 \qquad y \geqslant 3$$

(ii) Write down the points in this region with integer coefficients.

(iii) What happens to the number of viable integer points if all the inequalities are changed to $\leqslant$ or $\geqslant$?

9 **(i)** On the same axes, draw suitable graphs to maximise $C = x + y$ subject to

$2x + 3y \leqslant 12$

$3x + 2y \leqslant 15$

$x \geqslant 0$

$y \geqslant 0$

(ii) Name the points in this region with integer coefficients.

(iii) Use your graph to find the maximum value of C.

10 Solve the following problem graphically.

Minimise $x - 3y$ subject to $x - y \geqslant 5$ and $2x + 3y \leqslant 6$.

11 Gail and Anna are playing a tennis match. Gail plays a lob shot where her point of contact with the ball is 1 m above ground level and Anna returns the shot when it is descending and is 2.2 m above ground level. The ball's height h m at time t seconds after Gail hits it is given by $h = 1 + 20t - 5t^2$.

(i) Find the values of t when $h = 2.2$.

(ii) Find, to 2 decimal places, the length of time for which $h \geqslant 2.2$.

(iii) Show that during this time $h \leqslant 21$.

12 **(i)** On separate diagrams, use shading to illustrate each of the following inequalities.

    (a) $2x + 3y \leqslant 6$ **(b)** $2x + 3y \geqslant -6$

    (c) $2x - 3y \leqslant 6$ **(d)** $2x - 3y \geqslant -6$

(ii) Now transfer all the sketches onto a single diagram and state what shape is obtained.

13 **(i)** Use appropriate shading to illustrate the inequalities $y < x + 1$, $2x + y > 1$ and $x \leqslant 3$.

(ii) List all points with integer coefficients in the feasible region.

14 A boy wishes to stock a fishpond with c carp and t tench, subject to the following conditions.

- There must be at least 6 tench.

- There must be at least 4 carp.

- The total number of fish must not exceed 14.

- The number of tench must be greater than the number of carp.

  Using c to denote the number of carp and t to denote the number of tench, graph these inequalities with c on the horizontal axis and t on the vertical axis and mark all the points that represent possible purchases with crosses.

15 A family decides to have c cats and d dogs. Write the following statements as inequalities.

- Each of the 4 children must have at least one pet.

- The father refuses to have 8 or more pets in the house.

- The mother insists that the cats outnumber the dogs.

- They must have at least one dog to guard the house.

- The neighbours will complain if there are more than 5 cats.

Graph these inequalities and mark all possible combinations with crosses.

Exercise 7.2 Using inequalities for problem solving and linear programming

1 A small furniture company makes tables and chairs. A table requires 1.5 hours of machine time and 2 hours of assembly time. A chair requires 1 hour of machine time and 45 minutes of assembly time. In a week, there are, at most, 60 hours of machine time available and, at most, 60 hours available for assembly. The company must produce at least 8 tables and 16 chairs during a week.

   The graph below shows the feasible region, R, for the number of tables, x, and the number of chairs, y, that can be made during a week.

   Write the four inequalities shown on the graph and state how they relate to the information in the question.

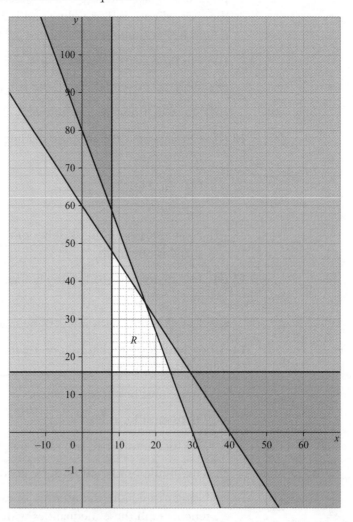

2 Amélie is a master chocolatier. She makes exquisite chocolates in her small shop in Paris. She produces two different boxes of chocolates: Luxury and Premium.

   The Luxury box contains 4 praline chocolates and 6 ganache chocolates. The Premium box contains 12 praline chocolates and 10 ganache chocolates.

   In any one day she must use at least 200 praline chocolates and at least 250 ganache chocolates but no more than 1600 chocolates in total. She is committed to supply a local hotel with at least 20 Luxury boxes per day.

   The graph on the next page shows the feasible region, R, for the number of Luxury boxes, x, and the number of Premium boxes, y, that can be made during a day.

Write the five inequalities shown on the graph and state how they relate to the information in the question.

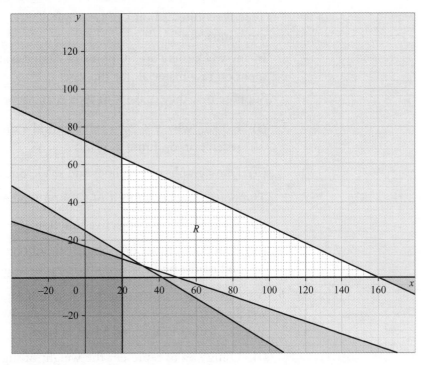

3 A local school is putting on a concert in order to raise money to sponsor a guide dog. The school hall seats a maximum of 500 people and tickets are to be priced at £12 each or £5 for children and concessions. To encourage children to attend, it is decided that at least one third of the tickets available should be priced at £5.

   (i) Using *a* to represent the number of £12 tickets and *c* to represent the number of £5 tickets, write down all inequalities that need to be satisfied, and illustrate the region satisfied by these, using the horizontal axis for *a* and the vertical axis for *c*.

   (ii) Write down the objective function for the total income £*P*.

   (iii) Find the maximum income possible under these constraints.

4 A toy company makes both dolls' prams and dolls' pushchairs, which use the same wheels and logo stickers. Each pram requires 4 wheels and 3 stickers, and each pushchair requires 4 wheels and 2 stickers. They have 2000 wheels and 1200 stickers available.

   Use *x* to represent the number of prams and *y* to represent the number of pushchairs.

   (i) Explain why $x + y \leqslant 500$ and find another similar inequality.

   (ii) Draw a suitable diagram and shade it to indicate the feasible region.

   Prams sell for £100 each and pushchairs for £70 each.

   (iii) Write down the objective function for the total income £*C* from sales and add the direction of this line to your graph.

   (iv) Find the number of each to maximise the income and hence the maximum income available per month.

5 A local pottery is making two types of large vases for sale.

Type A requires 1 hour of labour and costs £2 in raw materials.

Type B requires 2 hours of labour and also costs £2 in raw materials – it is more intricate.

In any week there are 80 hours of labour available and up to £120 can be spent on raw materials for the vases.

Suppose that they make x of type A and y of type B per week.

(i) Explain why $x + 2y \leqslant 80$ and find a similar inequality from the restriction on funds available.

(ii) Draw graphs of two lines and shade outside the feasible region.

The pottery makes a profit of £15 on type A and £25 on type B.

(iii) Write down the objective function.

(iv) Find the number of each that should be made to maximise the profit and hence find the maximum profit available.

6 A recipe for jam states that the weight of sugar used must be between the weight of fruit used and four-thirds of the weight of fruit used. Georgia has 10 kg of fruit available and 11 kg of sugar.

(i) Using s kg to represent the weight of sugar and f kg to represent the weight of fruit, formulate inequalities to model this information.

(ii) Draw a graph to represent your inequalities.

(iii) Find the vertices of your feasible region and identify the points which would represent the best mix of ingredients under each of the following circumstances.

    (a) There is to be as much jam as possible, given that the weight of jam produced is the sum of the weights of the fruit and the sugar.

    (b) There is to be as much jam as possible given that it is to have the lowest possible proportion of sugar.

    (c) There is to be as much jam as possible given that it is to have the highest possible proportion of sugar.

    (d) Fruit costs £4 per kg, sugar costs £1 per kg and the objective is to produce as much jam as possible within a budget of £32.

7 A haulage company has to transport 2000 packages using a combination of large vans which can take 300 packages each and small vans which can take 100 packages each. The cost of running each large van is £200 and the cost of running each small van is £100. The total cost must not exceed £1800. How can this be achieved minimising the cost?

8 Trigonometric functions

Exercise 8.1 Sine and cosine rules

1 Find the length x in each of the following triangles, giving your answer correct to 1 decimal place.

(i)

(ii)

2 Find the angle θ in each of the following triangles, giving your answer correct to 1 decimal place.

(i)

(ii)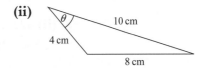

3 Find the area of each of the following triangles, giving your answer correct to 1 decimal place.

(i)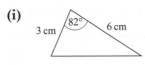

(ii)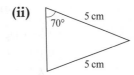

4 A triangle has adjacent sides of lengths 5 cm and 10 cm and an area of 15 cm².

   (i) Find the angle between the adjacent sides.

   (ii) Find the length of the third side.

5 A triangle ABC has AC = 7 cm, BC = 8 cm and angle BAC = 80°.

   (i) Sketch the triangle ABC.

   (ii) Find the angle at B.

   (iii) Find the length of AB.

6 A rhombus ABCD has sides of length 8 cm. The angle at A is 60°. Sketch the rhombus and find its area.

7 The diagonals of a parallelogram have lengths 8 cm and 12 cm and the acute angle between them is 60°.

   (i) Sketch the parallelogram.

   (ii) Find the lengths of the sides of the parallelogram.

8 In triangle ABC, BC = 8 cm, AC = 5 cm and angle BAC = 60°. Using c to represent the length of side AB

   (i) show $c^2 - 5c - 39 = 0$

   (ii) calculate the length of AB.

9 Solve the triangle ABC (i.e. find the remaining angle and sides) given that A = 26°, B = 82° and c = 6.7 cm.

10 The points P, Q and R have coordinates $(-1,-2)$, $(2,4)$ and $(8,7)$ respectively.

   (i) Find the lengths of the sides of triangle PQR.

   (ii) Find the angles of triangle PQR using the cosine rule.

   (iii) Show that you can use the gradients of the sides to obtain the same answers for the angles.

Exercise 8.2 Trigonometrical identities

1 Prove the identity $(1 - \sin x)(1 + \sin x) \equiv \cos^2 x$.

2 (i) Use the identity $\tan\theta = \dfrac{\sin\theta}{\cos\theta}$ to rewrite the equation $2\sin\theta = \cos\theta$ in terms of $\tan\theta$.

   (ii) Hence solve the equation $2\sin\theta = \cos\theta$ for $-180° \leqslant \theta \leqslant 180°$, giving your answers correct to 1 decimal place.

3 (i) Use the identity $\sin^2\theta + \cos^2\theta = 1$ to rewrite the equation $\sin^2\theta = 2\cos^2\theta - 1$ in terms of $\cos\theta$.

   (ii) Hence solve the equation $\sin^2\theta = 2\cos^2\theta - 1$ for $0° \leqslant \theta \leqslant 360°$, giving your answers correct to 1 decimal place.

4 The diagram shows part of the curves $y = \sin x$ and $y = 2\cos x$ which intersect at A.

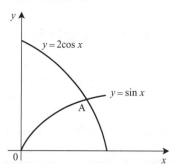

Find the coordinates of A.

5 (i) Show that $\cos^2 x - \sin^2 x = 2\cos^2 x - 1$.

   (ii) Find an expression for $\cos^2 x - \sin^2 x$ that does not involve $\cos x$.

6 (i) Show that $3\cos^2 x + 5\sin^2 x = 3 + 2\sin^2 x$.

   (ii) What are the greatest and least possible values of $3\cos^2 x + 5\sin^2 x$?

7 Use a suitable identity to solve $2\sin^2 x = 5\cos x + 4$ for $0° \leqslant x \leqslant 360°$.

8 Use a suitable identity to solve $\sin^2 x = 2\cos^2 x$ for $0° \leqslant x \leqslant 360°$, giving your answers correct to 1 decimal place.

9 Prove the identity $\tan x\sqrt{1 - \sin^2 x} \equiv \sin x$.

10 Prove the identity $\dfrac{\sin x\left(1 - \cos^2 x\right) - \cos x(1 - \sin^2 x)}{\cos^3 x} \equiv \tan^3 x - 1$.

Applications of trigonometry

Exercise 9.1 Applications of trigonometry in 2D

1   From a port P, two ships R and S are on bearings of 315° and 092°
    respectively. The distance PR = 8 km and the distance PS = 6.8 km.

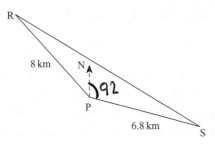

Find the distance between the ships, giving your answer correct to
1 decimal place.

2   A vertical tower CD stands on horizontal ground. The angle of elevation of
    the top of the tower, D, from a point A is 12°. Point B is on the straight line
    from A to C, the base of the tower, and AB = 100 m. The angle of elevation
    of the top of the tower from B is 25°. Giving your answers correct to
    1 decimal place, calculate

    (i) ∠ADB

    (ii) AD

    (iii) the height of the tower.

3   The shape of a new country's flag is
    a parallelogram. The diagram shows
    it on a flagpole. The lengths of its
    sides are 10.3 m and 7.2 m, and the
    acute angle between them is 80°.
    The flag is black with white lines
    along the diagonals. Find

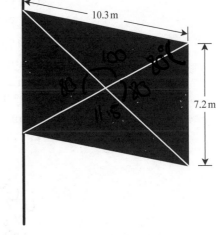

    (i)   the distance of the outside edge
             of the flag from the flagpole

    (ii) the total length of the white
             lines on the flag

    (iii) the area of the flag.

4   The diagram shows a village green bordered by
    three straight roads. The road PQ runs due north.

    (i) Find the bearing of R from Q to the nearest
            degree.

    (ii) Find the area of the village green to the nearest
            square metre.

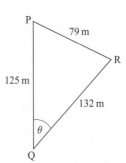

5   A yacht sets off from A and sails 4 km on a bearing
    of 076° to a point B then 3 km on a bearing of
    215° to a point C. How far is it from its starting point?

6 A tower 85 m high stands on the top of a hill. From a point on the ground at sea level, the angles of elevation of the top and the bottom of the tower are 45° and 25° respectively.

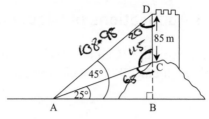

Find the height of the hill to the nearest metre.

7 A walker at point A can see the spires of St. Benedict's (B) and St. Cuthbert's (C) on bearings of 330° and 037° respectively. He then walks 400 m due north to a point D, from which the bearings are 310° and 084° respectively. Assume that all measurements are exact and that they are made in the same horizontal plane.

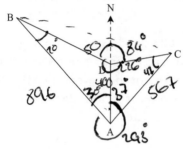

(i) Copy the diagram and add all the information from the question.

(ii) Calculate the distance AB to the nearest metre.

(iii) Given that the distance AC is 567 m, calculate BC, the distance between the spires, to the nearest metre.

8 At 12:00 the captain of a ship at a point A observes that the bearing of a lighthouse is 340°.

At 12:30 he takes another bearing of the lighthouse and finds it to be 030°. During this time the ship moves on a constant course of 280° to the point B.

His plot on the chart is shown below.

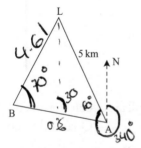

(i) Write down the size of the angles ∠LAB and ∠LBA.

(ii) The captain believes that at A he is 5 km from L. Assuming that LA is exactly 5 km, show that LB is 4.61 km, correct to 2 decimal places, and find AB, also correct to 2 decimal places.

(iii) Hence calculate the speed of the ship to 1 decimal place.

9 A helicopter leaves a point P and flies on a bearing of 217° for 15 km to a point Q, and then due East to a point R which is on a bearing of 150° from P.

    (i) Draw a diagram to show this information.

    (ii) Find PR.

    (iii) Find QR.

    (iv) The total flying time is 30 minutes. Find the speed of the helicopter.

10 From a point A on level ground, a skier can see the first station, B, of a ski lift at an angle of elevation of 30° and the next station, C, at an angle of elevation of 50°. The distance AB is 500 m and BC is 400 m.

    (i) Draw a diagram to show this information.

    (ii) Find ∠ACB.

    (iii) Find the distance AC.

    (iv) Calculate the gradient of BC.

Exercise 9.2 Applications of trigonometry in 3D

1 The jewellery box shown in the diagram is in the shape of a cuboid with sides of length 12 cm, 9 cm and 5 cm.

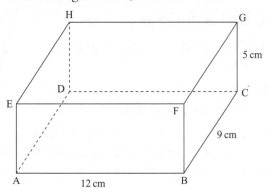

    (i) Find the length of AC.

    (ii) Find the angle that AG makes with the base ABCD.

    (iii) Find the length AF.

    (iv) Find the angle that AG makes with the front ABFE.

2 A door wedge is in the shape of a prism, with dimensions as shown in the diagram.

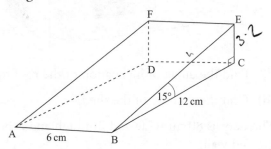

    (i) Find the length CE.

    (ii) Find the volume of wood in the wedge.

    (iii) What is the maximum number of such wedges that can be made from a block of wood 10 cm by 30 cm by 2 m?

3 A perfume bottle is made in the shape of a square-based pyramid, with the vertex directly above the centre of the base, and has dimensions as shown in the diagram.

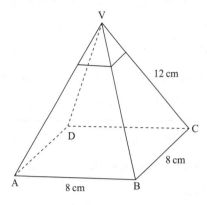

    (i) Find the angle between a slant edge and the base.

    (ii) Find the angle between a side and the base.

4 A vase has a square base ABCD of side 10 cm and a square top EFGH of side 15 cm. The vertical height of the vase is 20 cm.

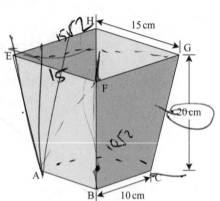

    (i) Find the length AC.

    (ii) Find the length EG.

    (iii) Find the length of the sloping edge AE.

    (iv) Calculate the angle of inclination of a sloping side to the horizontal.

5 The diagram shows a lean-to shed which is used to store garden equipment and materials. The base of the shed is 2 m by 4 m and the height is 2 m at the front and 3 m at the back.

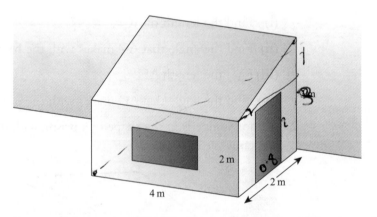

    (i) Find the angle of inclination of the roof to the horizontal.

    (ii) Find the volume of the shed.

The door is 80 cm wide and 2 m high and is positioned in the middle of the end wall.

    (iii) Find the length of the longest metal rod that can be stored in the shed.

6 Mollie is an advanced skier who is able to ski straight down a 100 m run on a slope inclined at 15° to the horizontal. James is a novice who can only ski down slopes inclined at 5°, so he needs to go across the slope as indicated in the diagram.

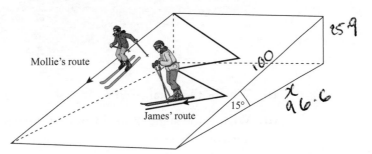

By considering the ski slope as a wedge, find

(i) the vertical fall of the 100 m run

(ii) the distance skied by James in getting from the top to the bottom, assuming James skies in a straight line across the slope.

7 A small dog kennel, as shown in the diagram, is built from plywood to the following dimensions.
- The rectangular base is 50 cm wide and 80 cm deep.
- The vertical sides are of height 50 cm.
- The front and back are 70 cm high at the apex.
- The entrance is 30 cm wide, with vertical sides and a semi-circular top and is 40 cm tall at its highest point.

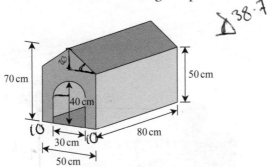

(i) Find the angle of inclination of the roof to the horizontal.

(ii) Find the volume of the kennel.

(iii) Find the area of wood removed for the entrance.

The roof is to be covered in roofing felt at a cost of £2.70 per square metre.

(iv) Using your answer to part **(i)**, calculate the lengths of the sloping sides of the roof and hence the cost of roofing felt required.

8 The diagram shows a swimming pool, ABCDEFGH, and its dimensions.

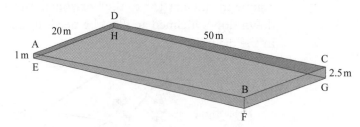

(i) What is the distance EF?

(ii) What is the angle of inclination of the base of the pool to the horizontal?

(iii) Melanie is only 1.2 m tall from her feet to her nose and walks from E towards F. How far is she from the shallow end before she cannot breathe?

(iv) How far can she walk if she goes directly from E to G?

(v) What is the volume of water in the pool in litres when it is full?

9 Jon is presenting the news on television while seated at his desk in the studio. The TV camera runs on a horizontal track which is suspended from the ceiling and the camera is at a height of 2.2 m above the floor and 3 m horizontally away from Jon. The camera track is 4 m long and Jon is seated opposite the centre of the track. Jon's eye level when seated is 1.25 m above the floor.

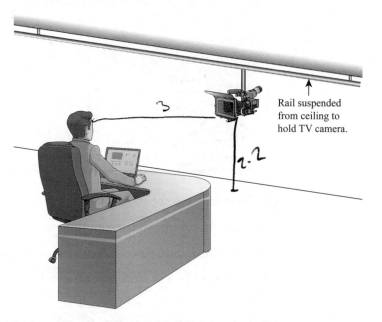

Rail suspended from ceiling to hold TV camera.

Giving distances to 2 decimal places and angles to 1 decimal place, find

(i) the least and greatest distances between Jon's eyes and the camera

(ii) the range of angles between Jon's line of sight and the horizontal, assuming that he is looking directly at the camera.

10 Nina is walking along a straight coastal path at sea level, and is at the point A in the diagram, when she notices that the angle of elevation of the top of the lighthouse is 5°. After walking a further 200 m she reaches the point B and notices that the angle of elevation is now 6°. The top of the lighthouse is 80 m above sea level.

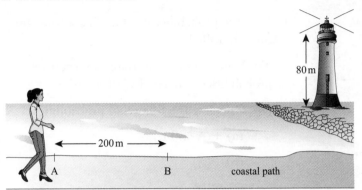

(i)   Giving all answers to the nearest metre, find the distances from each of the points A and B to the top of the lighthouse.

By first calculating suitable angles, calculate

(ii) how much further she needs to walk before she is directly opposite the base of the lighthouse

(iii) how far the base of the lighthouse is from the coastal path.

10 Permutations and combinations

Exercise 10.1 Probability diagrams

1 Find the probability of obtaining a total greater than 7 when two ordinary dice are rolled.

2 The Venn diagram illustrates the events A and B and some of the probabilities associated with them.

(i) Calculate the following probabilities.

(a) P(A and B)

(b) P(A)

(c) P(B)

(ii) Calculate P(A) × P(B) and hence show that A and B are independent events.

3 A fair tetrahedral die, with faces numbered 1, 2, 3 and 4, is rolled twice and the downward facing numbers added.

(i) Draw a sample space table to illustrate the possible sums.

(ii) Write down the probability of a sum of 5.

(iii) Write down the probability of a sum of 1.

4 Three people play a game which requires them to take turns rolling an ordinary die. Each player can only participate in the game once they have rolled a 6.

(i) Complete the tree diagram.

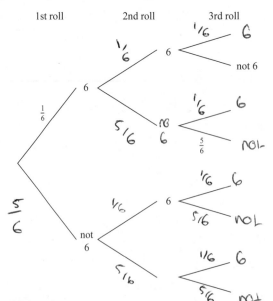

(ii) Work out the probability that in all of the first three rolls the die lands on a 6.

(iii) Work out the probability that on at least two of the first three rolls the die lands on a 6.

5 The table shows part of the distribution of a theatre audience.

	Balcony	**Box**	**Circle**	**Stalls**	**Total**
Children	31	21	96	187	335
Adults	58	23	101	109	291
Total	89	44	197	296	626

(i) Copy and complete the table.

(ii) A member of the audience is chosen at random.
Find the probability that the person is in a box.

(iii) Two members of the audience are chosen at random.
Find the probability that they are both adults from the circle.

6 A bag contains 5 red marbles, 3 blue marbles and 1 green marble.
Two marbles are chosen at random without replacement.

(i) Draw a probability tree diagram to illustrate the possible outcomes.

(ii) Find the probability that the green marble is one of the two chosen marbles.

(iii) Given that the green marble is one of the chosen marbles, calculate the probability that the other marble is blue.

7 The Venn diagram illustrates the events A, B and C, and some of the probabilities associated with them.

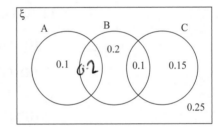

(i) Which two events are mutually exclusive?

(ii) Find the probability that both events A and B occur.

(iii) Hence, show that events A and B are not independent.

8 When facing a penalty taker, a goalkeeper chooses a direction to dive at random.

- She dives to her left with a probability of 0.5.
- She dives to her right with a probability of 0.4.
- She stays in the middle with a probability of 0.1.

The penalty taker chooses a direction to kick the ball at random.

- She kicks to the keeper's left with a probability of 0.6.
- She kicks to the keeper's right with a probability of 0.3.
- She kicks it down the middle with a probability of 0.1.

A goal is scored only if the keeper chooses a different direction to that in which the ball is kicked.

(i) Draw a probability tree diagram to illustrate the possible outcomes.

(ii) Calculate the probability that a goal is scored.

(iii) Given that a goal is scored, calculate the probability that the ball was kicked to the keeper's left.

9 A bag contains 8 red and 4 blue counters. A counter is removed at random. If the counter is blue then no more counters are removed.

If the counter is red then another counter is removed.

If the second counter is blue then no more counters are removed.

If the second counter is red then a third counter is removed.

   (i) Find the probability of removing at least one red counter.

   (ii) Find the probability of removing a blue counter.

10 Two events A and B are such that P(A) = 0.3 and P(neither A nor B) = 0.2.

   (i) Given that A and B are mutually exclusive, find P(B).

   (ii) Given, instead, that A and B are independent, find P(B).

11 Two bags contain red and blue marbles. Bag A contains 5 reds and 2 blues. Bag B contains 2 reds and 3 blues. A normal die is rolled and then two marbles are removed from a bag. If the number rolled is less than 5, then the two marbles are removed from bag A. If the number rolled is a 5 or a 6, then the two marbles are removed from bag B.

   (i) Calculate the probability of choosing two marbles of the same colour.

   (ii) Given that the two marbles are of the same colour, find the probability that they are both blue.

12 Two independent events A and B have probabilities x and y respectively.

   (i) Given that $P(A \text{ and } B) = \frac{1}{3}$, write down an equation in x and y.

   (ii) Given also that $P(A \text{ or } B) = \frac{23}{28}$, write down another equation in x and y.

   (iii) Given also that $x > y$ find the probabilities of A and B.

13 The probability of a hockey team winning a particular game is $\frac{3}{5}$.

   The probability that the reserve goalkeeper plays for the team is $\frac{2}{5}$.

   The probability that the team wins this particular game, given that the reserve goalkeeper plays is $\frac{1}{3}$.

   Calculate the following probabilities.

   (i) P(the team wins the game and the reserve goalkeeper plays)

   (ii) P(the team wins the game and the reserve goalkeeper does not play)

   (iii) P(the reserve goalkeeper does not play and the team does not win)

Exercise 10.2 Permutations and combinations

1 How many ways are there of arranging the letters of the word **M A T H S** ?

2 Calculate the value of $_9C_7$.

3 Write $_7P_3$ in the form $\frac{a!}{b!}$.

4 When an ordinary die is rolled four times, how many different outcomes are possible?

5 How many ways are there of awarding 4 different prizes to 4 people chosen from a group of 10?

6 How many ways are there of choosing a group of 5 players from a squad of 11?

7 Solve $_nP_2 = 72$.

8 A six-digit code is made up of a multiple of 12, followed by a prime number between 10 and 50, and then finally a two-digit square number.

    (i) How many different codes are possible?

    (ii) If the multiple, the prime, and the square can be in any order, how many different codes are possible?

9 Three normal dice are rolled. Find the probability that the sum of the three scores is less than 15.

10 A group comprises 5 men and 9 women.
Find the number of different sub-groups of 6 people that can be chosen if

    (i) there are no restrictions

    (ii) the sub-group must include all 5 men

    (iii) the sub-group must include at least 5 women.

11 Find how many arrangements of the letters **E D U C A T I O N** there are if

    (i) there are no restrictions on the order of the letters

    (ii) they must start with **E** and finish with **N**

    (iii) the letters **E** and **N** must be next to each other

    (iv) the letters **E** and **N** must not be next to each other.

12 Solve $2 \times {}_xP_{x-3} = {}_{x+1}P_{x-3}$.

13 Alan and Linda are in a group of 10 people sitting in a circle. Two arrangements are only considered to be different if the positions of the people are different relative to each other.

    (i) How many different arrangements of the 10 people are possible?

    (ii) In how many of these arrangements will Alan and Linda be sitting next to each other?

11 The binomial distribution

Exercise 11.1 Binomial expansion

1 Expand and simplify $(3 - y)^4$.

2 Expand $(1 + 2x)^5$, simplifying each of the terms.

3 Find the first three terms in the expansion of $(2 - 5y)^{10}$ in ascending powers of y.

4 Find the first three terms in the expansion of $(3 + 2w)^{12}$ in descending powers of w.

5 Expand $(1 - x)^8$ in ascending powers of x, up to the term in x^3, and simplify your answer.

6 In the expansion of $(2 + x)^9$ find the coefficient of the x^4 term.

7 In the expansion of $(4 - 3x)^7$ find the coefficient of the x^5 term.

8 In the expansion of $\left(3x^2 - \dfrac{2}{x}\right)^{12}$ find the term which is independent of x.

9 (i) Write down the expansion of $(a + b)^3$.

   (ii) Hence find the simplified expansion of $(x + 2y)^3$.

   (iii) By substituting 1 for a and $(x + 2y)$ for b in your answer to part (i), expand and simplify $(1 + x + 2y)^3$.

10 $1024y^{10}$ and $15360xy^9$ are two terms in the expansion of $(ax + by)^n$.

   (i) Find the positive integers a, b and n.

   (ii) Hence find the coefficient of the x^2y^8 term.

Exercise 11.2 Binomial distribution

1 The random variable X is given by $X \sim \mathrm{B}(6, 0.4)$. Calculate the following probabilities.

   (i) $\mathrm{P}(X = 0)$ (ii) $\mathrm{P}(X = 1)$ (iii) $\mathrm{P}(X \neq 1)$

   (iv) $\mathrm{P}(X < 2)$ (v) $\mathrm{P}(X \geq 2)$ (vi) $\mathrm{P}(X = 7)$

2 An ordinary die is rolled six times. Find the probability of rolling exactly three 5s.

3 43% of a school's students travel to the school by bus.
   A group of ten students is selected at random.
   Find the probability that the group will include exactly three students who travel by bus.

4 The random variable Y is given by $Y \sim \mathrm{B}\left(8, \dfrac{2}{3}\right)$.
   Calculate the following probabilities.

   (i) $\mathrm{P}(Y = 6)$ (ii) $\mathrm{P}(4 \leq Y \leq 5)$ (iii) $\mathrm{P}(Y > 1)$

5 John claims that he can tell the difference between two different drinks with similar tastes.

He blindfolds himself and randomly samples six of the drinks. He correctly states the name of the drink for five of the six.

If John is simply guessing, find the probability of correctly guessing at least five of the six drinks.

6 A die is biased so that the probability of rolling a six is 0.25
The die is rolled 7 times. Calculate the probability of obtaining

  (i) exactly 1 six

  (ii) at least 2 sixes.

7 A box contains a large number of tulip bulbs which all look alike. When the bulbs grow, some will produce red flowers and the others will produce yellow flowers. The red and yellow tulip bulbs are in the proportion 5 : 3 respectively. Seven bulbs are selected. Calculate the following probabilities.

  (i) P(all seven are yellow)

  (ii) P(exactly five are yellow)

8 A factory manufactures plates; it is known that 3% of the plates are defective. The plates are packed in boxes of ten. The contents of each box are independent of other boxes.

  (i) Calculate the probability that a randomly selected box contains at least one plate with a defect.

  (ii) Two boxes are selected. Calculate the probability that exactly one of the boxes contains a defective plate.

9 Given $X \sim B(5, p)$ and $P(X = 5) = 0.00243$, find $P(X = 3)$.

10 (i) Describe the circumstances under which a variable X has a binomial distribution.

  (ii) Give an example of such a situation and explain how the variable fulfils the requirements.

12 Exponentials and logarithms

Exercise 12.1 Exponentials and logarithms

1 **(i)** Sketch the graph of $y = 4^x$. Include the coordinates of any axis intercepts.

   (ii) Write down an equation of the asymptote.

2 Solve $\log_x 64 = 3$.

3 Write the expression 2^{3x+4} in the form $a \times b^x$ where a and b are integers to be determined.

4 The graphs of $y = 2^x$, $y = 3^x$, $y = \left(\dfrac{1}{2}\right)^x$ and $y = 2 \times 3^x$ are shown in the diagram.

   Match each graph to its equation.

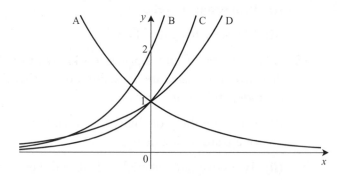

5 Given $\log_x (y + 2) = 5$, write y in terms of x.

6 The temperature, $\theta\,°C$ of a cup of tea is given by the formula $\theta = 20 + 65 \times 0.9^t$, where t minutes is the time since the tea was poured.

   (i) Find the temperature of the tea when it was poured.

   (ii) Find its temperature after 10 minutes.

7 Write each of these expressions as a single simplified logarithm.

   (i) $\log_a (3x) + \log_a (5y)$ **(ii)** $3 + \log_2 x$ **(iii)** $\log_4 2 \times \log_a (9w^2)$

8 Given $3^{y-4} = 7x$, write y in terms of x.

9 Solve $3^x = 16$, giving your answer correct to four significant figures.

10 The growth of a bacterial population is thought to follow a model of the form $M = a \times b^t$, where M is the mass (milligrams) of the bacteria and t is the number of days since the records began.

   (i) Show that the suspected relationship can be written as
   $\log_{10} M = \log_{10} a + t \log_{10} b$.

   The following data are collected.

t (days)	0	0.5	1	1.5	2	2.5	3
M (mg)	4.9	7.0	10.1	14.9	19.7	28.1	42.0

2·1   3·1   4·8   4·8   8·

(ii) Copy the axes shown and plot the points as $\log_{10} M$ against t.

(iii) Draw a line of best fit for the points plotted in part **(ii)**.

(iv) Hence, calculate estimates for the values of a and b.

(v) Use the model to estimate the mass when $t = 4$.

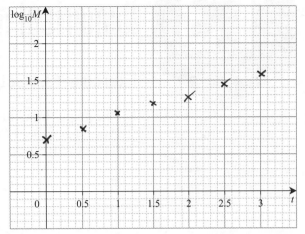

11 The mass, $m\,\mathrm{kg}$, of an ice sculpture is given by the formula $m = \dfrac{60}{1.1^t}$, where t is the time in hours measured from the time the sculpture is revealed.

(i) Find the mass of the sculpture when it is revealed.

(ii) Find its mass (to the nearest gram) after 2 hours.

(iii) The sculpture is revealed at 1pm. At what time will its mass be $30\,\mathrm{kg}$?

12 Solve $\log_2(x + 3) = 1 + \log_2 x$.

13 Two variables, x and y, are thought to be related by the formula $y = kx^n$ where k and n are unknown constants.

(i) Show that the relationship can be written as $\log_{10} y = \log_{10} k + n \log_{10} x$.

The following data are collected.

x	1.0	1.5	2	2.5	3.0	3.5	4.0
y	3.9	11.0	22.6	29.5	62.4	91.7	127.9

(ii) Copy the axes and plot the data as $\log_{10} y$ against $\log_{10} x$.

(iii) It is suspected that one of the results has been measured incorrectly. Identify the outlier.

(iv) Ignoring the outlier, draw a line of best fit for the remaining points.

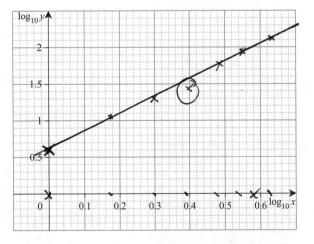

(v) Hence calculate estimates for the values of k and n, and write a formula for y in terms of x.

14 Solve $2^{3x} = 3^{x+1}$.

15 Solve $\log_2(x) + \log_2(x - 6) = 4$.

13 Numerical methods

Exercise 13.1 Solutions of equations, including iteration

1 The graph shows the curve $y = x + \log_{10} x$.
   Prove that a root of the equation $x + \log_{10} x = 0$ lies in the interval $0.1 < x < 0.5$.

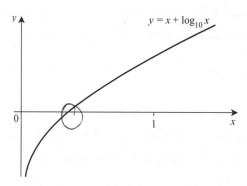

2 Using the sequence $x_{n+1} = \dfrac{x_n}{2} - 1$ with $x_0 = 6$ determine the values of x_1, x_2 and x_3.

3 The graph shows the curve $y = 3^x - 4x$.

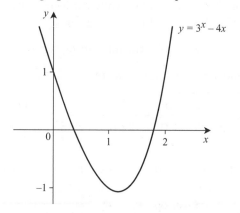

   (i) Prove that a root of the equation $3^x - 4x = 0$ lies in the interval $1.6 < x < 2$.

   (ii) Use interval bisection to find an interval of width 0.1 that contains the root.

4 Given that the sequence $x_{n+1} = 3 - \dfrac{x_n}{3}$ converges, use algebra to determine its limit.

5 The graph shows the curve $y = x^4 + x - 1$.

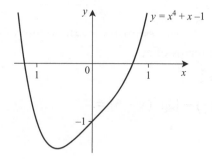

   (i) Prove that a root of the equation $x^4 + x - 1 = 0$ lies in the interval $0.7 < x < 0.8$.

(ii) Use a decimal search to find a root interval of width 0.001.

(iii) Write down the root to two decimal places.

6 An iterative sequence is given by $x_{n+1} = 3 - \dfrac{x_n}{2}$.

(i) Starting with $x_0 = 10$, find the values of x_1, x_2 and x_3.

(ii) Given that the sequence converges, use algebra to prove that its limit must be 2.

7 The graph shows the curve $y = \sqrt[3]{x} - x + 1$.
Prove that $x = 2.3$ is a root of the equation $\sqrt[3]{x} - x + 1 = 0$, correct to 1 decimal place.

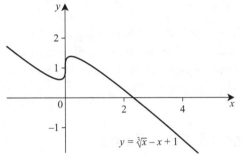

8 (i) Rearrange $x^3 - 2x + 3 = 0$ into the form $x = \sqrt[3]{ax + b}$ where a and b are constants to be determined.

(ii) Hence find a root (correct to two decimal places) of the equation $x^3 - 2x + 3 = 0$.

9 An iterative sequence is given by $x_{n+1} = \dfrac{3}{2^{x_n}}$.

Copy the graphs of $y = x$ and $y = \dfrac{3}{2^x}$.

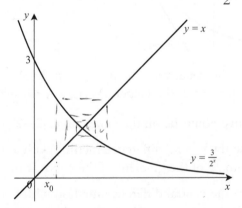

(i) Draw a cobweb/staircase diagram to illustrate the behaviour of the sequence when $x_0 = 0.5$, identifying the terms x_1, x_2 and x_3 on the x-axis.

(ii) Find the root of the equation $x = \dfrac{3}{2^x}$ correct to one decimal place.

10 The equation $x = \dfrac{x^3 + 1}{3} - x^2 + x$ has three roots: α, β and γ, where $\alpha < \beta < \gamma$.

Matthew wishes to use the iterative sequence $x_{n+1} = \dfrac{(x_n)^3 + 1}{3} - (x_n)^2 + x_n$ to find α, β and γ.

(i) Use the sequence to find one of the roots correct to 4 decimal places.

The graphs of $y = x$ and $y = \dfrac{x^3 + 1}{3} - x^2 + x$ are shown in the diagram.

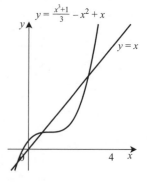

(ii) Which root(s) cannot be found using the sequence?

(iii) Copy the graphs. Then, using a suitably chosen x_0, demonstrate the divergent nature of the sequence. Label the positions of x_0 and x_1 on the x-axis.

Exercise 13.2 Gradients

1 The graph shows the curve $y = 2^x - 3$ and the tangent at $(2, 1)$.

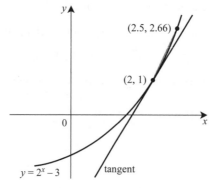

Use the chord between the points $(2.5, 2.66)$ and $(2, 1)$ to find an estimate of the gradient of the tangent. Write your answer to 1 d.p.

2 These five points lie on the same curve: $(2, -2)$, $(3, -1)$, $(4, 2)$, $(5, 8)$ and $(6, 18)$.

(i) Use the central difference method with a step of 1 to calculate an estimate of the gradient of the curve at the point $(4, 2)$.

(ii) Use the central difference method with a step of 2 to calculate another estimate of the gradient of the curve at the point $(4, 2)$.

(iii) Which of these estimates is more reliable, and why?

3 A tangent to the graph of $y = \log_{10} x$ is drawn at the point $(10, 1)$.

(i) Use a forward difference method with a step of 2 to calculate an estimate of the gradient of the tangent.

(ii) Use a forward difference method to calculate a more reliable estimate. Show your method clearly.

(iii) Why is your answer to part **(ii)** more reliable?

4 These four points lie on the same curve: (1,3), (2,6), (3,4) and (4,1).

   (i) Use the central difference method to calculate an estimate of the gradient of the curve at the point (2,6).

   (ii) Use the central difference method to calculate an estimate of the gradient of the curve at the point (3,4).

   (iii) Use a forward difference method with a step of 1 to calculate an estimate of the gradient of the curve at the point (1,3).

   (iv) Use a backward difference method with a step of 1 to calculate an estimate of the gradient of the curve at the point (4,1).

5 The displacement (in metres) of a motorbike from a point P is given by the formula $x = 2^t - 1$ for $0 \le t \le 5$ where t is measured in seconds.

   (i) Use a forward difference method to calculate an estimate of the motorbike's initial velocity. Use a step of 0.2 seconds and give your answer in km h^{-1} to one decimal place.

   (ii) Use a central difference method to calculate an estimate of the motorbike's velocity after 3 seconds. Use a step of 0.2 seconds and give your answer in km h^{-1} to one decimal place.

6 The driver of a car spots a hazard in the road and decides to stop his car. While he is braking, his velocity (in metres per second) is given by $v = \dfrac{20}{2^t} - 1$ where t is measured in seconds.

   (i) Calculate the car's velocity (in metres per second) after 2 seconds.

   (ii) Calculate the time taken (in seconds) to stop the car, to two decimal places.

   (iii) Use a central difference method to calculate an estimate of the car's deceleration (in metres per second^2) after 2 seconds. Use a step of 0.1 seconds. Give your answer correct to three significant figures.

Exercise 13.3 Areas

1 The graph shows the curve $y = 1 + 2\sqrt{x}$.

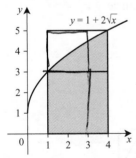

Use the rectangles to show that the shaded area, A, satisfies the inequality $9 < A < 15$.

2 The graph shows the curve $y = 9 - x^2$.

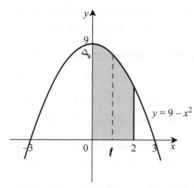

Use the trapezium rule with two strips to estimate the area enclosed by the curve, the x-axis, the y-axis and the line $x = 2$.

3 The graph shows the curve $y = 3 - \sqrt[3]{x}$.

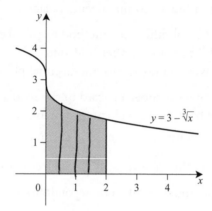

(i) Use the trapezium rule with four strips to find an estimate of the shaded area enclosed by the axes, the line $x = 2$ and the curve, giving your answer to three decimal places.

(ii) Will the answer to part (i) be an underestimate or an overestimate of the shaded area?

4 The graph shows the curve $y = 36 - x^2$.

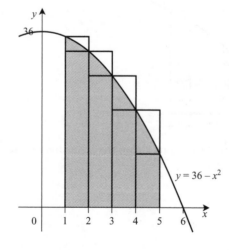

Using the rectangles shown in the diagram, calculate lower and upper bounds for the shaded area enclosed by the curve, the x-axis and the lines $x = 1$ and $x = 5$.

5 A region is enclosed by the curve $y = 2^x$, the x-axis, and the lines $x = 1$ and $x = 5$.

   (i) Use the trapezium rule with eight strips to estimate the area of the region.

   (ii) Briefly explain how a better estimate can be calculated.

6 Using the trapezium rule with four strips, estimate the area bounded by the x-axis, the lines $x = 1$, $x = 7$ and the curve $y = 1 + 2\log_{10} x$.

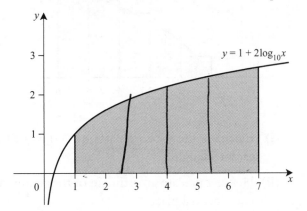

7 An athlete competes in a short race. Her velocity (in metres per second) is given by $v = 3\log_{10}(t + 1)$ for $0 \leqslant t \leqslant 10$ seconds. A velocity–time graph is drawn.

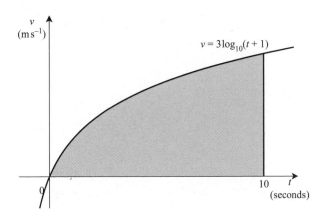

   (i) Using the trapezium rule with five strips, estimate the shaded area.

   (ii) Briefly explain the significance of the answer to part **(i)**.

8 The area bounded by the x-axis, the line $x = 6$ and the graph of $y = 3\log_{10} x$ is estimated using five rectangles of width 1. Each rectangle is drawn such that the graph passes through the midpoint of one of its sides as shown.

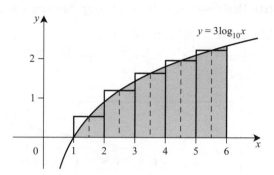

(i) Calculate the y-coordinates (to 3 d.p.) of the five points at the top of each rectangle.

(ii) Hence calculate an estimate of the required area, giving your answer to two decimal places.

(iii) Will this be an overestimate or an underestimate?

14 Differentiation

Exercise 14.1 Differentiation

1 Differentiate each of the following functions with respect to x.

   (i) **(a)** $y = 2x^3$ **(b)** $y = 3x^4$ **(c)** $y = 4x^5$

   (ii) **(a)** $y = 2x^2 + x$ **(b)** $y = 3x^3 + 2x^2$ **(c)** $y = 4x^4 + 3x^3$

   (iii) **(a)** $y = \dfrac{x^3}{3} + \dfrac{x^2}{2}$ **(b)** $y = \dfrac{x^4}{3} + \dfrac{x^2}{2}$ **(c)** $y = \dfrac{x^6}{3} + \dfrac{x^4}{2}$

2 **(i)** Differentiate the following functions with respect to r.

      (a) $A = \pi r^2$ **(b)** $V = \dfrac{4}{3}\pi r^3$

   (ii) Use your answers to part **(i)** to write down a relationship between V and A.

3 Differentiate each of the following functions with respect to x.

   (i) $y = (2x + 3)(x + 1)$ **(ii)** $y = (x^2 + 1)(x - 1)$ **(iii)** $y = (4x + 1)^2$

4 The gradient of the curve $y = x^4 + kx^2 + 3$ at the point where $x = -1$ is -8. Find the value of k.

5 The function $f(x)$ is defined by $f(x) = (x - 1)(x^2 + 2)$.

   (i) Find $f'(x)$.

   (ii) Find $f'(-2)$.

6 The sketch shows the point $P(1,12)$ on the graph of $y = x^3 - 6x^2 + 2x + 15$.

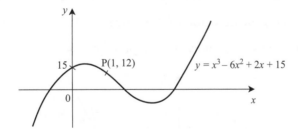

Find

   (i) the gradient function $\dfrac{\mathrm{d}y}{\mathrm{d}x}$

   (ii) the gradient of the curve at the point P

   (iii) the equation of the tangent to the curve at the point P

   (iv) the equation of the normal at the point P.

7 The sketch shows the point P(−1,−8) on the graph of $y = 9x - x^3$.

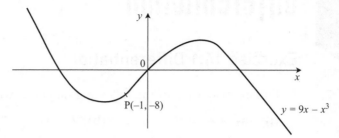

Find

(i) the gradient function $\dfrac{dy}{dx}$

(ii) the gradient of the curve at the point P

(iii) the equation of the tangent to the curve at the point P

(iv) the equation of the normal at the point P.

8 The sketch shows the graph of $y = x^3 - 3x^2 - 5$.

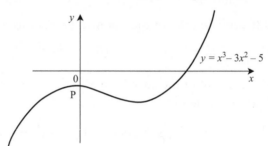

Find

(i) the gradient function $\dfrac{dy}{dx}$

(ii) the gradient of the curve at the point P where it crosses the y-axis

(iii) the equation of the tangent to the curve at the point P

(iv) the equation of the normal to the curve at the point P.

9 The sketch shows the graph of $y = x^3 - 3x$.

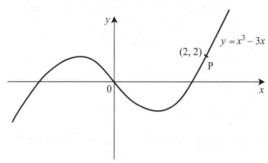

(i) Find the equation of the tangent to the curve at the point P(2,2).

(ii) Verify that the tangent meets the curve again at the point where $x = -4$.

(iii) Find the value of y at this point of intersection.

10 The sketch shows the graph of $y = (x - 3)(7 - x)$.

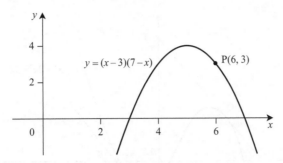

(i) Find the equation of the tangent to the curve at the point P(6,3).

(ii) Find the equation of the normal to the curve at P.

(iii) Verify that the normal passes through the origin.

11 A cubic curve has equation $y = x(x - 2)(x - 3)$.

(i) Find $\dfrac{\mathrm{d}y}{\mathrm{d}x}$.

(ii) Find the gradient of the curve at each of the points where it crosses the x-axis.

12 The sketch shows the graph of $y = x^3 - 2x^2 - 3x + 1$.

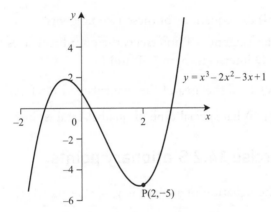

(i) Find the equation of the tangent at the point P(2,−5).

(ii) Find the coordinates of the point where this tangent meets the curve again.

13 The sketch shows the graph of $y = x^3 - 2x^2 - 4x + 3$.

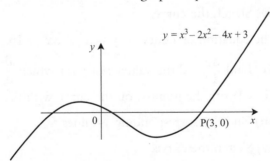

Find

(i) the equation of the tangent at the point P(3,0)

(ii) the x-coordinate of another point Q on the curve where the tangent at Q is parallel to the tangent at P.

14 The sketch shows the graph of $y = x^3 + 3x^2 - 7x - 4$.

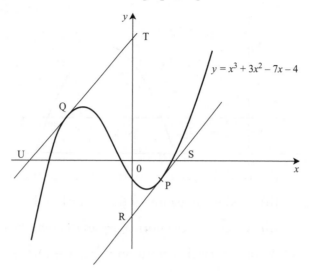

Find

(i) $\dfrac{dy}{dx}$

(ii) the coordinates of the points P and Q, given that the gradient of the tangent to the curve is 2 at both points

(iii) the equations of these two tangents.

The tangent at P intersects the coordinate axes at R and S and the tangent at Q intersects them at T and U.

(iv) Find the area of the quadrilateral RSTU.

(v) What special type of quadrilateral is this?

Exercise 14.2 Stationary points

1 The equation of a curve is $y = x^3 - 6x^2 + 4$.

(i) Find $\dfrac{dy}{dx}$ and the value(s) of x for which $\dfrac{dy}{dx} = 0$.

(ii) Classify the point(s) on the curve with these x-values.

(iii) Find the corresponding y-values.

(iv) Sketch the curve.

2 The equation of a curve is $y = x^4 - 8x^2 + 16$.

(i) Find $\dfrac{dy}{dx}$ and the value(s) of x for which $\dfrac{dy}{dx} = 0$.

(ii) Classify the point(s) on the curve with these x-values.

(iii) Find the corresponding y-values.

(iv) Sketch the curve.

3 The equation of a curve is $y = 9x + 3x^2 - x^3$.

(i) Find $\dfrac{dy}{dx}$ and the value(s) of x for which $\dfrac{dy}{dx} = 0$.

(ii) Classify the point(s) on the curve with these x-values.

(iii) Find the corresponding y-values.

(iv) Sketch the curve.

4 The equation of a curve is $y = x^4 - 4x^3 + 6$.

   (i) Find $\dfrac{dy}{dx}$ and the value(s) of x for which $\dfrac{dy}{dx} = 0$.

   (ii) Classify the point(s) on the curve with these x-values.

   (iii) Find the corresponding y-values.

   (iv) Sketch the curve.

5 For each of the curves given below

      (a) $y = x^2 - 3x + 2$

      (b) $y = x^3 - 3x^2 + 2x$

   (i) find $\dfrac{dy}{dx}$ and the value(s) of x for which $\dfrac{dy}{dx} = 0$

   (ii) classify the point(s) on the curves with these x-values and find the corresponding y-values.

   (iii) Sketch both curves on the same axes.

6 A curve has equation $y = x^3 - 2x^2 - 4x + 3$.

   (i) Find the coordinates of the stationary points and distinguish between them.

   (ii) Sketch the curve.

7 A curve has equation $y = 3x^3 + ax^2 + bx + 4$. When $x = 1$, $y = 5$ and $\dfrac{dy}{dx} = 2$.

   (i) Using the information given, write down two equations involving a and b and solve them simultaneously.

   (ii) Show that the curve has no stationary points.

8 Find the position and nature of the stationary points of the curve $f(x) = x^3 + 2x^2 - 4x + 3$.

9 The graph of $y = x^3 - 3x^2 + px + q$, where p and q are constants, passes through the point $(2, -12)$ and its gradient at that point is -9.

   (i) Find the values of p and q.

   (ii) Find the coordinates of the stationary points of the function and distinguish between them.

   (iii) Sketch the curve.

10 A function is said to be 'increasing' when $\dfrac{dy}{dx} > 0$ and 'decreasing' when $\dfrac{dy}{dx} < 0$. For the function $f(x) = x^3 - 3x + 4$

   (i) locate and classify the turning points of the curve

   (ii) sketch the curve

   (iii) determine the ranges of values of x for which $f(x)$ is an increasing function

   (iv) determine the range of values of x for which $f(x)$ is a decreasing function.

11 The curve $y = ax^3 - 3x + 2b$ has a turning point at the point with coordinates (a,b) where $a > 0$.

   (i) Use the fact that (a,b) is on the curve to write down a first equation connecting a and b.

   (ii) Use the fact that (a,b) is a turning point to write down a second equation.

   (iii) Solve these equations to find a and b.

   (iv) Prove that the turning point (a,b) is a minimum.

12 The curve $y = a + bx^3 + cx^4$ has a maximum turning point at $(-2,20)$ and a point of inflection at $(0,4)$.

   (i) Use the fact that these points are on the curve to write down two equations connecting a, b and c.

   (ii) Use other information given in the question to write down a further equation connecting a, b and c.

   (iii) Solve these equations to find values for a, b and c.

   (iv) Sketch the curve.

13 The diagram shows a rectangular sheet of cardboard 8 cm by 5 cm. Equal squares of side x cm are cut from each corner and the edges are then turned up to make an open box.

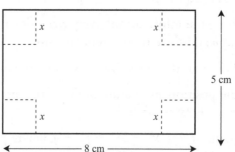

Denoting the volume of the box by $V\,\text{cm}^3$, show that $V = 4x^3 - 26x^2 + 40x$. Find the only viable stationary point and prove that it is a maximum.

15 Integration

Exercise 15.1 Introduction to integration

1. Find y in each of the following cases.

   (i) $\dfrac{dy}{dx} = 4x - 2$ **(ii)** $\dfrac{dy}{dx} = 3x^2 + 2x - 1$ **(iii)** $\dfrac{dy}{dx} = 5$

2. Find $f(x)$ given that

   (i) $f'(x) = x^3 - 3x^2 + 1$ **(ii)** $f'(x) = (x - 2)^2$

   (iii) $f'(x) = 4 - 2x$ **(iv)** $f'(x) = 4$

3. Find the following integrals.

   (i) $\displaystyle\int 3x^2 dx$ **(ii)** $\displaystyle\int \left(3x^2 + 2x\right) dx$

   (iii) $\displaystyle\int \left(3x^2 + 2x + 1\right) dx$ **(iv)** $\displaystyle\int 3\, dx$

4. **(i)** For each of the following gradient functions find the equation of the curve $y = f(x)$ that passes through the given point.

   (a) $\dfrac{dy}{dx} = 2x$; (1,3)   **(b)** $\dfrac{dy}{dx} = 2x$; (1,0)   **(c)** $\dfrac{dy}{dx} = 2x$; (1,–3)

   (ii) Sketch each of the curves in part **(i)** on the same axes and say what you notice.

5. **(i)** For each of the following gradient functions find the equation of the curve $y = f(x)$ that passes through the given point.

   (a) $\dfrac{dy}{dx} = 2x$; (3,1)   **(b)** $\dfrac{dy}{dx} = 2x$; (1,0)   **(c)** $\dfrac{dy}{dx} = 2x$; (–3,1)

   (ii) Sketch each of the curves in part **(i)** on the same axes and say what you notice.

6. Find the following integrals.

   (i) $\displaystyle\int (2x + 1)(x - 1)\, dx$ **(ii)** $\displaystyle\int (2x + 1)^2\, dx$ **(iii)** $\displaystyle\int (2x + 1)(x - 1)^2\, dx$

7. For each of the following gradient functions find the equation of the curve $y = f(x)$ that passes through the given point.

   (i) $\dfrac{dy}{dx} = 2x^2 + 4$; (2,7)   **(ii)** $\dfrac{dy}{dx} = x^2 + 1$; (–3,4)

   (iii) $f'(x) = (x + 1)^2$; (2,3)   **(iv)** $f'(x) = (x - 1)(x + 1)$; (3,2)

8. You are given that $\dfrac{dy}{dx} = 4x - 3$.

   (i) Find the general solution of the differential equation.

   (ii) Find the particular solution that passes through (−1,5).

9. The curve C passes through (4,−2) and its gradient function is given by $f'(x) = 3x^2 - 6x - 4$.

   (i) Find the equation of the curve.

   (ii) Find the coordinates of the points where the curve intersects the line $y = -2$.

10 The gradient function of a curve is $6x^2 - 6$. The curve has two stationary points, one a maximum with a y-value of 7 and the other a minimum with a y-value of -1.

  (i) Find the value of x at each stationary point.

  (ii) Find the equation of the curve.

  (iii) Sketch the curve.

11 The curve with gradient function $3x^2 - 2x - 1$ passes through the point $(2,3)$.

  (i) Find the equation of the curve.

  (ii) Find the coordinates of any stationary points for the curve.

  (iii) Sketch the curve.

12 A curve, C, has stationary points at the points where $x = 0$ and where $x = 2$.

  (i) Explain why $\dfrac{dy}{dx} = x^2 - 2x$ is a possible expression for the gradient of C.

  (ii) Give a different possible expression for the gradient function.

  (iii) The curve passes through the point $(3,2)$. Given that $\dfrac{dy}{dx} = x^2 - 2x$, find the equation of C.

Exercise 15.2 Definite integrals and areas

1 Evaluate the following.

  (i) $\left[\dfrac{x^3}{3}\right]_1^2$

  (ii) $\left[3x^2 + 2x\right]_0^3$

  (iii) $\left[x^3 + 2x\right]_{-2}^2$

2 Evaluate the following definite integrals.

  (i) $\displaystyle\int_0^2 4x \, dx$

  (ii) $\displaystyle\int_{-3}^3 x^2 \, dx$

  (iii) $\displaystyle\int_{-2}^4 (2x + 5) \, dx$

  (iv) $\displaystyle\int_{-3}^3 (9 - x^2) \, dx$

  (v) $\displaystyle\int_{-1}^1 (x + 1)(x - 1) \, dx$

  (vi) $\displaystyle\int_{-1}^1 x^3 \, dx$

3 Find the area of each of the shaded regions in the figure.

  (i)
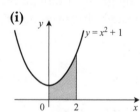

  (ii)
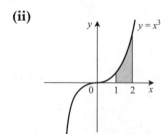

  (iii)
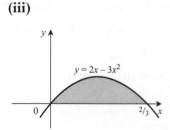

  (iv)
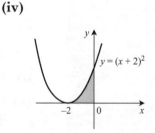

4 The sketch shows part of the curve $y = x^2 - 4$.

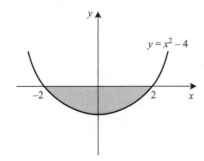

Calculate the area of the shaded region.

5 The sketch shows the curve $y = x^3 - 6x^2 + 8x$.

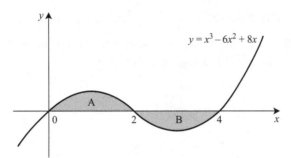

(i) Calculate each of the shaded areas A and B.

(ii) Evaluate $\int_0^4 (x^3 - 6x^2 + 8x)\,dx$

(iii) What do you notice?

6 (i) Sketch the curve $y = x^2 - 3x$ for $-1 \leqslant x \leqslant 4$.

(ii) For what values of x does the curve lie below the x-axis?

(iii) Find the area between the curve and the x-axis.

7 (i) Shade, on a suitable sketch, the region whose area is given by $\int_{-1}^3 (4 + x)(4 - x)\,dx$.

(ii) Find the area of the shaded region.

8 The sketch shows the graphs of the curve $y = x^2 - 4x - 4$ and the line $y = 2x + 3$ which intersect at the points A and B.

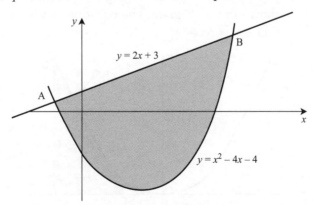

(i) Find the coordinates of A and B.

(ii) Find the area of the shaded region.

9 The sketch shows the graph of $y = 4 - x^2$ and the tangent to the curve at the point A(2,0).

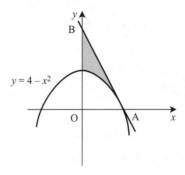

(i) Find the equation of the tangent AB.

(ii) Find the area of the shaded region.

10 A toy kite ABCD is constructed using the pattern in the diagram, where the y-axis is a line of symmetry.

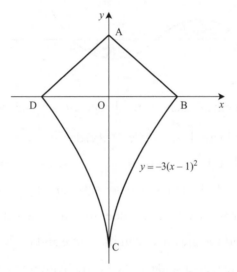

(i) Find the equation of the line AB.

(ii) Find the area of ABCD.

(iii) Find the area of the kite if 1 unit represents 40 cm.

11 A drainage ditch is being dug with a symmetrical cross-section ABCD as shown in the diagram. The equation of OC is $y = x^2$ and the equation of CD is $y = 5x - 4$.

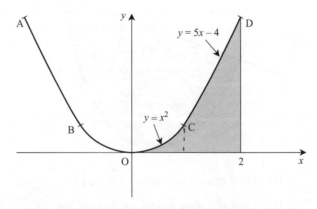

(i) Find the area of the shaded region.

(ii) Find the volume of earth removed in a 100 m length of ditch if 1 unit represents 50 cm.

16 Applications to kinematics

Exercise 16.1 Motion with constant acceleration

Throughout this exercise take the acceleration due to gravity as $9.8\,\mathrm{m\,s}^{-2}$ unless instructed otherwise.

1 Decide which *suvat* equation to use in each of these situations.

   (i) Given a, u, v find t.

   (ii) Given a, s, v find u.

   (iii) Given s, t, u find a.

   (iv) Given t, u, v find s.

2 **(i)** Find s when $u = 0$, $v = 5$, $t = 2$.

   (ii) Find t when $u = 2$, $v = 7$, $a = 0.4$.

   (iii) Find a when $u = -2$, $v = 4$, $s = 3$.

   (iv) Find v when $u = 3$, $a = -2$, $t = 3$ and interpret the result.

   (v) Find u when $s = 10$, $a = 3$, $t = 4$ and interpret the result.

3 A stone is dropped from a height of $8\,\mathrm{m}$.

   (i) How long does it take to reach the ground?

   (ii) How fast is it moving when it reaches the ground?

4 A ball is thrown vertically upwards from a point A with a speed of $12\,\mathrm{m\,s}^{-1}$ and later caught at the same point A. Find the length of time for which the ball is in the air.

5 What acceleration, in $\mathrm{m\,s}^{-2}$, is needed to increase the speed of a car from rest to $5\,\mathrm{m\,s}^{-1}$ in 4 seconds?

6 A car accelerates uniformly from a speed of $36\,\mathrm{km\,h}^{-1}$ to a speed of $81\,\mathrm{km\,h}^{-1}$ in 10 seconds as it travels along a straight road.

   (i) Calculate the acceleration of the car in $\mathrm{m\,s}^{-2}$.

   (ii) Calculate the distance travelled in that time, giving your answer to the nearest metre.

7 A firework rises vertically from the ground to a height of $100\,\mathrm{m}$ in $5\,\mathrm{s}$. Assume that the firework starts from rest and has a constant acceleration.

   (i) Find its speed when it reaches a height of $100\,\mathrm{m}$.

   After $5\,\mathrm{s}$ the firework burns out and continues to move vertically under gravity.

   (ii) Find the maximum height reached by the firework.

   (iii) Find the total time that the firework is in the air.

8 An object moves along a straight line. It starts at the origin with a velocity of $8\,\mathrm{m\,s}^{-1}$ and has a constant acceleration of $-5\,\mathrm{m\,s}^{-2}$.

   (i) After how long is the object instantaneously at rest?

   (ii) How far from the origin is it at this time?

   (iii) When does it next pass through the origin?

   (iv) When is the object $1.5\,\mathrm{m}$ from the origin?

9 A tennis ball travelling vertically downwards with a speed of $5\,\mathrm{m\,s^{-1}}$ falls into a pond, where it experiences a deceleration of $2\,\mathrm{m\,s^{-2}}$.

   (i) Find the time the ball takes to come to rest.

   (ii) Find how far below the surface of the pond the ball is at that point.

   (iii) Assuming that the water resistance is constant, and that the ball is sufficiently buoyant to return to the surface with a uniform acceleration in $5\,\mathrm{s}$, find its speed when it reaches the surface.

10 An airport has a straight runway of length $2000\,\mathrm{m}$. During take-off a light aircraft, starting from rest and moving with a constant acceleration reaches its take-off speed of $120\,\mathrm{km\,h^{-1}}$ after 25 seconds.

   (i) Express the take-off speed in $\mathrm{m\,s^{-1}}$.

   (ii) Find the acceleration during take-off in $\mathrm{m\,s^{-2}}$.

   (iii) Find the fraction of the length of the runway used by the aircraft during take-off.

11 Two stones are thrown vertically upwards from the same place at 1 second intervals, with an initial speed of $15\,\mathrm{m\,s^{-1}}$. Taking g to be $10\,\mathrm{m\,s^{-2}}$

   (i) determine how long the first stone has been in the air when they collide

   (ii) find their velocities at the time of the collision.

Exercise 16.2 Motion with variable acceleration

1 **(i)** Given that $s = 5t^2$ find v when $t = 2$.

   (ii) Given that $v = 2t^2 + 3$ find a when $t = 3$.

   (iii) Given that $s = t^3 - 2t + 1$ find a when $t = 4$.

2 Given that $v = 2t + 3$ and $s = 6$ when $t = 1$, find

   (i) s in terms of t

   (ii) the initial displacement.

3 A body is initially at O. At time t its velocity is given by $v = 4t - 3t^2$.

   (i) Find a in terms of t.

   (ii) Find s in terms of t.

   (iii) What is the value of t when the body next passes O?

4 A particle starts from rest and moves along a straight line with acceleration $(6 + 6t)\,\mathrm{m\,s^{-2}}$. After $1\,\mathrm{s}$ it has travelled $10\,\mathrm{m}$.

   (i) Find v in terms of t.

   (ii) Find s in terms of t.

   (iii) Find the time when $v = 24$.

   (iv) Find s at that time.

5 The velocity of a moving object at time t seconds is given by $v\,\mathrm{m\,s^{-1}}$ where $v = 5t - t^2 - 6$.

   (i) Find the times when the object is instantaneously at rest.

   (ii) Find the acceleration at these times.

   (iii) What is the velocity when the acceleration is zero?

   (iv) Sketch the graph of v against t.

6 The height of a ball thrown vertically upwards is modelled by
$h = 14t - 4.9t^2 + 1$.

  (i) Find an expression for the velocity of the ball.

  (ii) What is the time when the ball reaches its maximum height?

  (iii) What is the maximum height reached?

  (iv) Find the acceleration of the ball and comment on your result.

7 A particle moves along a straight line and t seconds after passing through
the origin O its velocity is given by $v = c_1 t + c_2 t^2$ where c_1 and c_2 are
constants.

  (i) Find an expression in terms of c_1, c_2 and t for the acceleration of the
  particle.

  When $t = 2$ the body is again at O and has an acceleration of $6\,\mathrm{m\,s^{-2}}$.

  (ii) Use this to find an equation connecting c_1 and c_2.

  (iii) Find an expression for the displacement x m of the body at time t.

  (iv) Use this to find a second equation connecting c_1 and c_2.

  (v) Use the equations found in parts **(ii)** and **(iv)** to find the velocity in
  terms of t.

8 Ellie is 12 years old and can run at $6\,\mathrm{m\,s^{-1}}$. She has been entered for a 60 m
race. A model is proposed where she accelerates uniformly to her maximum
speed of $6\,\mathrm{m\,s^{-1}}$ in four seconds, and then runs at her maximum speed for
the rest of the distance. The diagram below shows the speed–time graph for
this model.

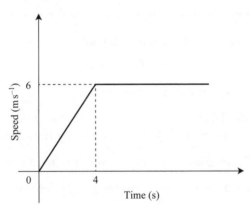

  (i) Find the distance run in the first four seconds.

  (ii) Find the total time taken to run the race.

  Her teacher suggests an alternative model whereby for the first four seconds
  her speed $v\,\mathrm{m\,s^{-1}}$ at time t seconds is given by the formula $v = \frac{3}{16}(6t^2 - t^3)$.

  (iii) Find v when $t = 4$.

  (iv) Show that the distance run in the first four seconds is the same as for
  the first model.

9 A skateboarder sets off from rest. His speed, t seconds after setting off, is $v\,\mathrm{m\,s^{-1}}$, where $v = t - 0.05t^2$.

(i) Find when he is next at rest.

(ii) Calculate his initial acceleration.

(iii) Find an expression for his displacement at time t.

(iv) Given that this is measured from his starting point, calculate how far he has travelled before he is next at rest.

(v) Sketch a velocity–time graph for $0 \leqslant t \leqslant 20$ and indicate how the distance in part (iv) is related to the graph.

10 The sketch shows part of the velocity–time graph for the motion of an insect walking in a straight line. Its velocity $v\,\mathrm{mm\,s^{-1}}$ at time t seconds is given by $v = 8 + 2t - t^2$.

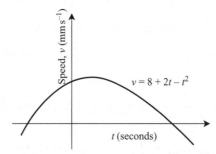

(i) Write down the velocity of the insect when $t = 0$.

(ii) Find when the insect is instantaneously at rest.

(iii) What happens next?

(iv) Find the maximum velocity of the insect.

(v) Calculate the distance travelled

   (a) in the first four seconds

   (b) in the first five seconds.

11 The displacement $x\,\mathrm{m}$ from the origin O of a particle on the x axis is given by $x = 4 + 8t + t^2 - t^3$, where t is the time in seconds and $0 \leqslant t \leqslant 4$.

(i) Write down the displacement when $t = 0$.

(ii) Find an expression, in terms of t, for the velocity $v\,\mathrm{m\,s^{-1}}$ of the particle.

(iii) Find an expression, in terms of t, for the acceleration $a\,\mathrm{m\,s^{-2}}$ of the particle.

(iv) Find the maximum velocity of the particle in the interval $0 \leqslant t \leqslant 4$.

(v) Find the value of t when $v = 0$ and also the value of x at this time.

(vi) Calculate the distance travelled by the particle in the first two seconds.

12 The velocity $v\,\mathrm{m\,s^{-1}}$ of a particle P at time t seconds is given by $v = t^3 - 4t^2 + 4t + 2$. P moves in a straight line.

(i) Find an expression for the acceleration, $a\,\mathrm{m\,s^{-2}}$, in terms of t.

(ii) Find the times at which the acceleration is zero, and say what is happening between these times.

(iii) Find the distance travelled in the first three seconds.

Full worked solutions to all of the questions can be found at www.hoddereducation.co.uk/OCRAddMathsExamPractice

1 Algebraic manipulation

Exercise 1.1 Simplifying algebraic fractions

1. (i) $\dfrac{4x}{3y}$

   (ii) $\dfrac{4x}{3y}$

   (iii) $\dfrac{4x}{3y}$

   (iv) $\dfrac{4x}{3y}$

2. (i) $\dfrac{3}{3x+2}$

   (ii) $\dfrac{x}{4y}$

   (iii) $\dfrac{a-2}{a+2}$

   (iv) $\dfrac{p-3}{3}$

3. (i) (a) $\dfrac{2x+3}{(x+1)(x+2)}$

      (b) $\dfrac{2x+5}{(x+2)(x+3)}$

      (c) $\dfrac{2x+7}{(x+3)(x+4)}$

   (ii) $\dfrac{x+5}{x+4} - \dfrac{x+4}{x+5} = \dfrac{2x+9}{(x+4)(x+5)}$

4. (i) $\dfrac{2y^2}{15x}$

   (ii) $\dfrac{2(x+1)}{(x+5)}$

   (iii) $\dfrac{3(p-2)}{p(p+3)}$

   (iv) $\dfrac{(2r+3)^3}{3r^4}$

5. (i) $\dfrac{5-2a}{a^2}$

   (ii) $\dfrac{19p}{9}$

   (iii) $\dfrac{5a}{6b}$

   (iv) $\dfrac{25p}{12q}$

6. (i) $\dfrac{20x}{3} + \dfrac{x^2}{4}$

   (ii) $\dfrac{29a}{12}$

   (iii) $x - 6x^2$

   (iv) $p^2 + 9p - \dfrac{34}{9p}$

7. (i) $\dfrac{9}{2x+1}$

   (ii) $\dfrac{3}{(3a-1)(a+2)}$

   (iii) $-\dfrac{p}{(p-1)(p-2)}$

   (iv) $\dfrac{5r^2+4r-3}{(r-1)(r+2)(r-3)}$

8. (i) $x = 3$

   (ii) $p = 5$

   (iii) $x = \dfrac{1}{3}$ or $x = 3$

   (iv) $x = 4$ or $x = -1$

9. $\dfrac{x-2}{x+3} = \dfrac{2}{3} \Rightarrow x = 12$

10. (i) True for one value, $x = 2$.

    (ii) True for all values of x.

    (iii) False

Exercise 1.2 Simplifying expressions containing square roots

1. (i) $\sqrt{6}$

   (ii) $2\sqrt{3}$

   (iii) $2\sqrt{5}$

   (iv) $2\sqrt{2}$

   (v) $2\sqrt{6}$

   (vi) $4\sqrt{3}$

2. (i) $2\sqrt{3}$

   (ii) $3\sqrt{5}$

   (iii) $4\sqrt{5}$

   (iv) $5\sqrt{6}$

3 (i) $3\sqrt{6}$

(ii) 4

(iii) $9 - 2\sqrt{3}$

(iv) $\sqrt{2}$

4 (i) $6 + 2\sqrt{2} + 3\sqrt{3} + \sqrt{6}$

(ii) $6 + 2\sqrt{2} - 3\sqrt{3} - \sqrt{6}$

(iii) $6 - 2\sqrt{2} + 3\sqrt{3} - \sqrt{6}$

(iv) $6 - 2\sqrt{2} - 3\sqrt{3} + \sqrt{6}$

5 (i) $13 - 3\sqrt{5}$

(ii) $2 + \sqrt{2}$

(iii) $52 - 14\sqrt{3}$

6 (i) $2\sqrt{2}$

(ii) $\dfrac{3\sqrt{2}}{2}$

(iii) $\dfrac{\sqrt{2}}{4}$

(iv) $\dfrac{\sqrt{3}}{3}$

(v) $\dfrac{\sqrt{10}}{2}$

7 (i) $x^2\sqrt{x}$

(ii) $2\sqrt{2}x\sqrt{x}$

(iii) $3\sqrt{3x}$

(iv) $xy\left(\sqrt{y} + \sqrt{x}\right)$

(v) $4\sqrt{3}x^3$

8 (i) $\sqrt{20}$

(ii) $\sqrt{128}$

(iii) $\sqrt{600}$

(iv) $\sqrt{432}$

9 (i) $\dfrac{4}{7}$

(ii) $\dfrac{5\sqrt{15}}{3}$

(iii) $\dfrac{2\sqrt{6}}{9}$

(iv) $\dfrac{\sqrt{6}}{5}$

10 (i) $\dfrac{x\sqrt{x}}{y^2}$

(ii) $\dfrac{6x\sqrt{x}}{y}$

(iii) $\dfrac{x\sqrt{6x}}{12y}$

(iv) $\dfrac{y\sqrt{7x}}{7x}$

11 (i) $5 - \sqrt{3}$

(ii) $\sqrt{5} - 5$

12 (i) 3

(ii) $9\sqrt{6} - 30$

(iii) $37 + 20\sqrt{3}$

(iv) $35 - 12\sqrt{6}$

13 (i) $x^2 - 9y$

(ii) $9x - 30\sqrt{xy} + 25y$

(iii) $9x + 30\sqrt{xy} + 25y$

(iv) $x^2\sqrt{y} - xy\sqrt{x}$

14 (i) $x = -3 \pm 2\sqrt{3}$

(ii) $x = \dfrac{1}{3}$ (repeated)

(iii) $x = \dfrac{3 \pm \sqrt{21}}{6}$ or $\dfrac{1}{2} \pm \dfrac{\sqrt{21}}{6}$

15 (i) $4\sqrt{5}$

(ii) $3\left(\sqrt{5} + \sqrt{2}\right)$

(iii) $= \dfrac{14 - 5\sqrt{3}}{11}$

16 (i) $\dfrac{\sqrt{xy}}{y}$

(ii) $\dfrac{x + 4y + 4\sqrt{xy}}{x - 4y}$

(iii) $\dfrac{4x + 9y + 12\sqrt{xy}}{4x - 9y}$

17 $x = 2\sqrt{5}$

18 $57.6\,\text{cm}^2$

19 (i) $\dfrac{3x}{\sqrt{2}}\,\text{cm}$

(ii) $240\,\text{cm}$

2 Polynomials, functions and equations

Exercise 2.1 Operations with polynomials

1 (i) 3

(ii) 5

(ii) 2

2 (i) $6x^3 + 7x^2 - 3x - 16$

(ii) $3x^3 - 3x^2 - 2x + 7$

3 **(i)** $x^3 + 3x^2 + 3x - 8$

(ii) $x^4 - x^3 - x^2 + 2x - 2$

4 **(i)** $2x^3 + 2x^2 - 4x + 6$

(ii) $4x^3 + 6x^2 - 12x + 20$

(iii) $x^3 - 1$

(iv) The answer to part **(iii)** is the same as the initial expression from part **(i)**.

5 **(i)** $x^3 + 4$

(ii) $x^3 - x^2 - 2x + 8$

(iii) $2x^3 - 3x + 2$

(iv) The answer to part **(iii)** is the same as the initial expression from part **(i)**.

6 **(i)** $6x^3 - 11x^2 - 3x + 2$

(ii) $6x^6 + 10x^5 + 2x^4 - 9x^2 - 15x - 3$

7 **(i)** $18x^5 - 12x^4 + 2x^3 - 27x^2 + 18x - 3$

(ii) $x^4 - 8x^2 + 16$

8 **(i)** $x^2 + 3x + 2$

(ii) $x^2 - 3x + 2$

9 **(i)** $x^2 + 5$

(ii) $2x^2 - 4x + 9$

10 **(i)** $x^4 - 4x^3 - 12x^2 + 32x + 64$

(ii) $x^2 - 2x - 8$

(iii) $(x + 2)^2 \times (x - 4)^2 = (x^2 - 2x - 8)^2$

11 **(i)** $2x^3 - 6x^2 + 12x - 9$

(ii) $2x^2 - 2x$

12 **(i)** $x^3 - 12x^2 + x + 2$

(ii) $5x^3 - 4x^2 + 18x - 22$

Exercise 2.2 The factor theorem, completing the square and the quadratic formula

1 **(i)** This is a 'show that' question, so a short answer cannot be given here. See the full worked solution online.

(ii) $(x - 1)(x^2 - x - 6)$

(iii) $(x - 1)(x + 2)(x - 3)$

2 **(i)** Factors: $\pm 1, \pm 2, \pm 4, \pm 8$
$(x - 2)(x^2 - x + 4)$

(ii) Factors $\pm 1, \pm 3$
$(x + 3)(x^2 + 1)$

(iii) Factors $\pm 1, \pm 2, \pm 3, \pm 6$
$(x + 2)(2x + 1)(x + 3)$

3 **(i)** $2x^2 + 7x + 1$

(ii) This is a 'show that' question, so a short answer cannot be given here. See the full worked solution online.

4 $a = 2$ or $a = 3$

5 $a = 5, b = 2$, other factor $= (x + 4)$

6 $x = -2, \dfrac{1}{2}$ or 3

7 **(i)** Only (b)

(ii) $4x^3 - x^2 - 28x - 20$

(iii) $4x^2 - 9x - 10$

(iv) Although individually the expressions are not all divisible by $(x + 2)$, their sum is.

8 **(i)** $x = 3 \pm \sqrt{7}$

(ii) $x = 3 \pm \sqrt{11}$

(iii) $x = -3 \pm \sqrt{7}$

(iv) $x = -3 \pm \sqrt{11}$

9 **(i)** $x = 3$ or $x = 1$

(ii) $x = 2 \pm \sqrt{7}$

(iii) $x = -1$ or $x = -3$

(iv) $x = -2 \pm \sqrt{7}$

10 **(i)** $(x - 1)(x - 1)(x + 3)$

(ii) A is $(-3,0)$
B $= (1,0)$
C $= (0,3)$

(iii) $\left(2\dfrac{1}{3}, 9\dfrac{13}{27}\right)$.

11 **(i)** **(a)** $(x - 2)$ is a factor.

(b) $(x - 3)$ is a factor.

(ii) $(x - 2)(x - 3)(x + 5)$

(iii) $x = 2$ or, 3 or -5

12 **(i)** $h = \dfrac{18}{x^2}$ metres

(ii) This is a 'show that' question, so a short answer cannot be given here. See the full worked solution online.

(iii) This is a 'show that' question, so a short answer cannot be given here. See the full worked solution online.

(iv) $(x - 3)$ is a factor.

(v) Dimensions: $3\,\text{m} \times 3\,\text{m} \times 2\,\text{m}$
or $3.62\,\text{m} \times 3.62\,\text{m} \times 1.37\,\text{m}$

13 This is a 'show that' question, so a short answer cannot be given here. See the full worked solution online.

14 (1.83, 4.65) and (−2.63, −4.25)

3 Applications of equations and inequalities in one variable

Exercise 3.1 Applications of equations

1 10

2 10 cm

3 −8, −7 or 7, 8

4 4.5 cm and 5.5 cm

5 2 cm × 2 cm and 4 cm × 4 cm

6 $t = 1.09$ seconds

7 (i) 177 mm (nearest mm)

(ii) 188 mm × 177 mm (nearest mm)

8 4 m s^{-1} horizontally

Exercise 3.2 Linear and quadratic inequalities and their illustrations

1 (i) $x > -2$

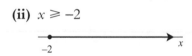

(ii) $x \geq -2$

(iii) $x < -2$

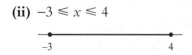

(iv) $x \leq -2$

2 (i) $-3 < x < 4$

(ii) $-3 \leq x \leq 4$

(iii) $x < -3$ or $x > 4$

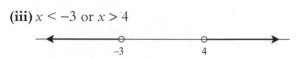

(iv) $x \leq -3$ or $x \geq 4$

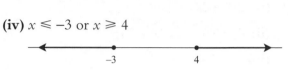

3 (i) $-2 < x < 0.5$

(ii) $x < -2$ or $x > 0.5$

(iii) $-2 \leq x \leq 0.5$

(iv) $x \leq -2$ or $x \geq 0.5$

4 (i) $-3 \leq x \leq 2$

(ii) $2 < x < 5$

(iii) $x \leq -1$ or $x \geq 4$

(iv) $x < -3$ or $x > 4$

5 $1 < x < 2$

6 $0 < x < 5$

7 (i)

(ii)

(iii)

(iv)

8 (i) $x > 1$

(ii) $x = \dfrac{1 + \sqrt{5}}{2}$

9 (i) $x = -1$ or $x = 7$

(ii)

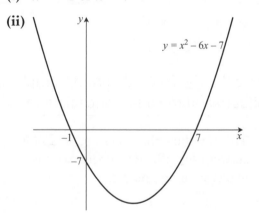

(iii) $-1 \leq x \leq 7$

(iv)

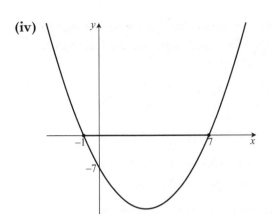

10 (i) $x = \frac{1}{3} \pm \frac{\sqrt{10}}{3} = 1.39$ or $\frac{1}{3} + \frac{\sqrt{10}}{3} = -0.72$

(ii)

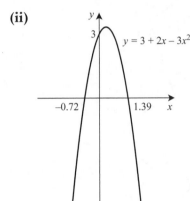

$y = 3 + 2x - 3x^2$

(iii) $-0.72 < x < 1.39$

(iv)

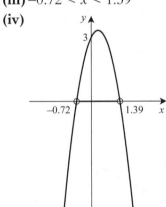

4 Sequences and recurrence relationships

Exercise 4.1 Sequences and recurrence relationships

1 (i) $0, 3, 6, 9$
AP with $a = 0, d = 3$

(ii) $0, -3, -6, -9$
AP with $a = 0, d = -3$

(iii) $0, -3, 0, -3$
Oscillating

(iv) $0, 3, 0, 3$
Oscillating

2 (i) $2, -2, -10, -26, -58$

(ii) $2, -2, -2, -10, -34$

(iii) $2, -2, -10, -14, 2$

(iv) $2, -2, 2, -2, 2$

3 (i) $6, 0, 12, -12$

(ii) $6, 12, 0, 24$

(iii) $6, 0, 18, -36$

(iv) $6, 12, -6, 48$

4 (i) $1, 1, 1, 1$

(ii) $-1, -5, -17, -53$

(iii) $0, -2, -8, -26$

5 $0, 18, 995$

6 (i) $a = 3, b = 2$

(ii) $u_3 = 3^3 - 2^3 + 4 = 23$

(iii) 669

7 (i) $0, 2, 4, 6$

(ii) $0, 2, 4, 6$

(iii) Both sequences have the same numerical values.

(iv) This is a 'prove that' question, so a short answer cannot be given here. See the full worked solution online.

8 (i) $1, 5, 1, 5, 1$

(ii) (a) $-1, 11, -13, 35$
Oscillating and increasing in magnitude

(b) $2, 3.5, 2.75, 3.125$
Oscillating with a limit of 3

9 (i) This is a 'show that' question, so a short answer cannot be given here. See the full worked solution online.

(ii) $\sqrt{6}$

(iii) $x_n = \sqrt{5x_{n-1} + 1}$

(iv) 5.19 (2 d.p.)

10 (i) This is a 'show that' question, so a short answer cannot be given here. See the full worked solution online.

(ii) $x = 0.3222$ (4 s.f.)

(iii) $(0.3222)^3 + 3(0.3222) - 1 = 4.85 \times 10^{-5}$

(iv) Using $x_1 = 0$ and the rearrangement $x = \sqrt[3]{1 - 3x}$ gives 1, ... oscillating between -1.64 and 1.81 (3 s.f.)

11 (i) 4%

(ii) £328 983

(iii) 18 years

12 (i) $p_{n+1} = 0.9p_n$

(ii) (a) £19 440

(b) £14 172

(iii) (a) £19 548

(b) £14 370

5 Points, lines and circles

Exercise 5.1 Points and lines

1 (i) $1\frac{1}{3}$

(ii) $-\frac{3}{4}$

(iii) 10

(iv) $(2,7)$

2 (i) (a) 5

(b) 10

(c) 15

(ii) (a) $1\frac{1}{3}$

(b) $1\frac{1}{3}$

(c) $1\frac{1}{3}$.

(iii) O, P and Q lie on a straight line through $(0,0)$ and with gradient $1\frac{1}{3}$, (i.e., the line $y = \frac{4x}{3}$).

3 (i) This is a 'show that' question, so a short answer to the first part cannot be given here. Eqn of the line is $x - 3y + 13 = 0$

(ii) $\frac{\sqrt{13}}{2} = 1.80$ (3 s.f.)

4 $c = -3$

5 This is a 'show that' question, so a short answer cannot be given here. See the full worked solution online.

6 $(3, 2 + 2\sqrt{3})$ or $(3, 2 - 2\sqrt{3})$

7 $(3,0)$

8 (i) (a) $(0,-6)$ and $(2,0)$

(b) $(0,1)$ and $(-5,0)$

(c) $(0,2)$ and $(3,0)$

(ii) Segment (c) is the shortest.

(iii)

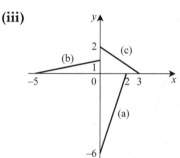

9 (i)

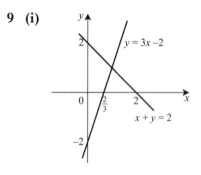

$(1,1)$

(ii)

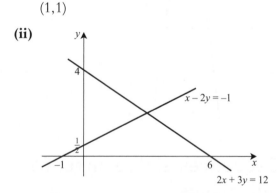

$(3,2)$

(iii)

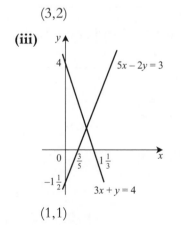

$(1,1)$

10 (i)

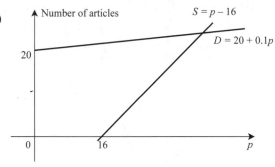

(ii) Equilibrium price = £40
Number bought (D) = 24
Number sold (S) = 24

11 (i)

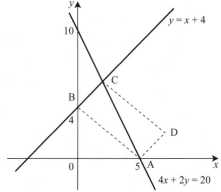

(ii) A(5,0)   B(0,4)   C(2,6)

(iii) 4 square units

(iv) (7,2)

Exercise 5.2 Circles

1 (i) $(x-1)^2 + (y-1)^2 = 4$

(ii) $(x-2)^2 + (y-5)^2 = 9$

(iii) $(x+1)^2 + (y+4)^2 = 25$

2 (i) Radius = 2, centre = $(-1,2)$

(ii)

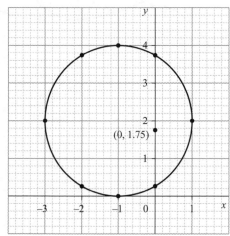

(iii) $(0,1.75)$ lies inside the circle

3 (i) $x^2 + y^2 = 25$

(ii) $(x-2)^2 + (y+3)^2 = 13$

(iii) $(x-0.5)^2 + (y-1)^2 = 31.25$

4 This is a 'show that' question, so a short answer cannot be given here. See the full worked solution online.

5 Origin lies inside the circle.

6 (i) Touches x-axis at (3,0)

(ii) Touches x-axis at (1,0) and y-axis at (0,−1)

(iii) Touches x-axis at (5,0) and y-axis at (0,5)

(iv) Touches y-axis at (0,−2)

7 (i) Line doesn't meet the circle.

(ii) Line is a tangent to the circle.

8 This is a 'show that' question, so a short answer cannot be given here. See the full worked solution online.

9 (i)

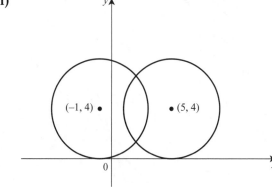

(ii) (2,1.35) and (2,6.65)

(iii) Line joining centres is $y = 4$ (horizontal).
Line joining points of intersection is $x = 2$ (vertical).
Angle between = 90°.

10 (i)

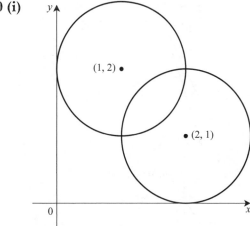

(ii) (1,1) and (2,2)

(iii) Line joining centres: $x + y = 3$
Line joining points of intersection: $y = x$
Angle between = 90°.

11 (i) AB = $2\sqrt{5}$
BC = $3\sqrt{5}$
AC = $\sqrt{65}$

(ii) Centre $= (2.5, 7)$
Radius $= \sqrt{16.25}$

(iii) $x^2 - 5x + y^2 - 14y + 39 = 0$

6 Graphs

Exercise 6.1 Cartesian graphs

1 (i)

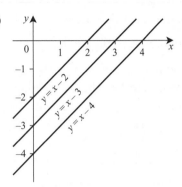

(ii)

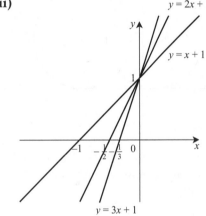

(iii)

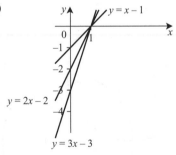

2 (i)

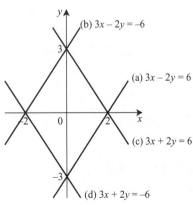

(ii) Rhombus

3 (i) $y = (x - 3)(x + 2)$

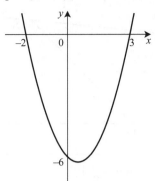

(ii) $y = (2x + 1)(x - 2)$

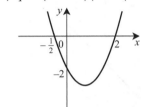

(iii) $y = (3x - 2)(x + 3)$

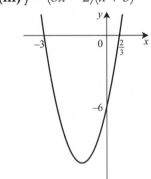

4 (i) (ii)

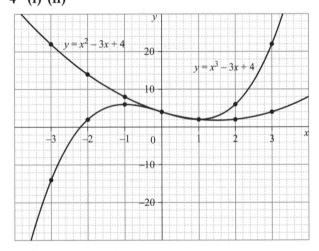

(iii) $(0, 4)$ and $(1, 2)$

(iv) Answer confirmed algebraically.

Answers

5 (i)

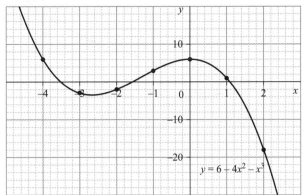

(ii) $x = 0$ or $x = -4$

(iii) Answer confirmed algebraically.

6 (i)

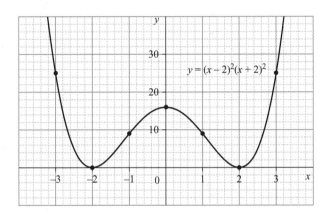

(ii) The curve has the y-axis as a line of symmetry.

(iii)

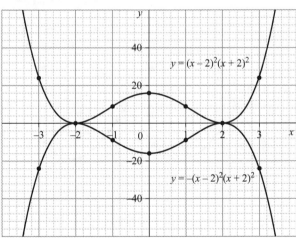

(iv) The combined graphs are symmetrical about both the x and y-axes.

7 (i)

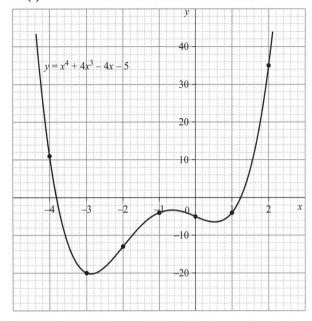

(ii) $(-1,-4)$, $(0,-5)$ and $(1,-4)$

8 (i)

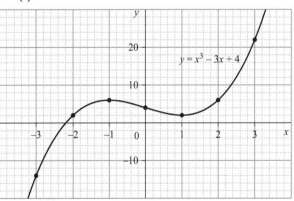

(ii) $(-\sqrt{3},4)$, $(0,4)$ and $(\sqrt{3},4)$

(iii) Rotational symmetry about $(0,4)$.

9 Through $(1, 1)$ and $(3,4)$, $y = 1.5x - 0.5$

Through $(3,4)$ and $(5,1)$, $y = -1.5x + 8.5$

Through $(5,1)$ and $(3,-2)$, $y = 1.5x - 6.5$

Through $(3,-2)$ and $(1,1)$, $y = -1.5x + 2.5$

10 (i) $y = (x - 1)(x - 3)(x - 5)$

(ii) $y = 4x(x - 3)^2$

(iii) $y = -2(x - 1)(x - 4)^2$

(iv) $y = -\dfrac{1}{9}(x + 1)^2(x - 4)^2$

Exercise 6.2 Trigonometric and exponential graphs

1 (i)

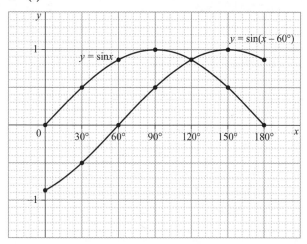

(ii) The graph of $y = \sin(x - 60°)$ is the same shape as the graph of $y = \sin x$ but translated $60°$ in the positive x-direction.

(iii) The graph of $y = \sin(x - 30°)$ is the same shape as the graph of $y = \sin x$ but translated $30°$ in the positive x-direction.

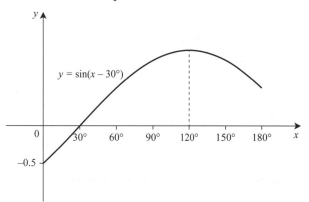

2 (i)

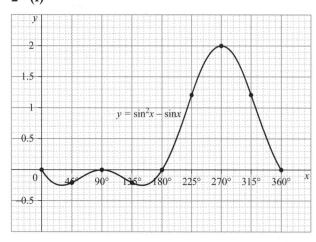

(ii) $x = 0°, 90°, 180°, 360°$

(iii) Solve $\sin^2 x - \sin x = 0$

3 (i)

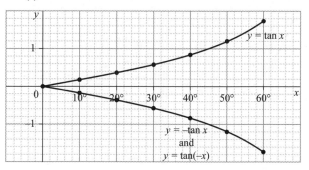

(ii) In this range $y = \tan(-x)$ and $y = -\tan x$ are reflections of $y = \tan x$ in the x-axis.

4 (i)

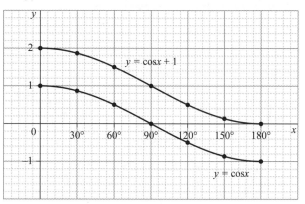

(ii) Both graphs have the same shape. $y = \cos x + 1$ is 1 unit above $y = \cos x$.

5 (i), (ii)

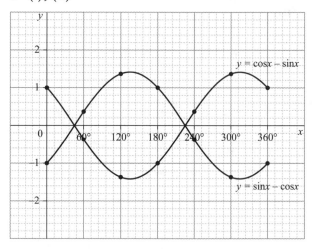

(iii) $y = \cos x - \sin x$ is the reflection of $y = \sin x - \cos x$ in the x-axis.

6 (i) $(-0.767, 0.588)$

(ii) (a)

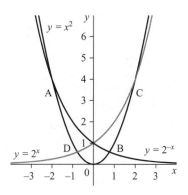

(b) $(-2, 4)$ and $(0.767, 0.588)$

7 (i) (b)

(ii) (d)

(iii) (c)

(iv) (a)

8 (i)

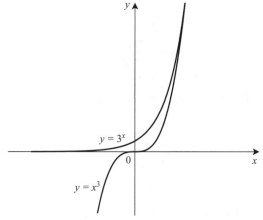

(ii) Similarities: In both graphs $y \Rightarrow \infty$ as $x \Rightarrow \infty$.

Differences: As $x \Rightarrow -\infty, 3^x \Rightarrow 0$ and $x^3 \Rightarrow -\infty$.

9 (i) (a) $y = 2^x$ and $y = 2^{-x}$ are reflections in the y-axis, both passing through $(0,1)$.

(b) $y = 3 + 2^x$ and $y = 3 - 2^x$ are reflections in the line $y = 3$; $y \to 3$ as $x \to -\infty$.

(c) $y = 3 + 2^{-x}$ and $y = 3 - 2^{-x}$ are also reflections in the line $y = 3$; $y \to 3$ as $x \to \infty$.

(ii)

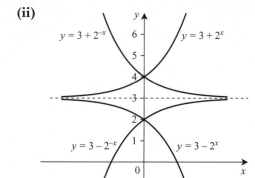

10 (i), (ii)

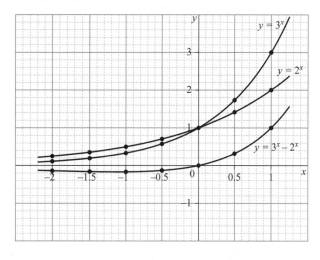

(iii) As $x \to -\infty$, $3^x - 2^x \to 0$ from negative values.

7 Linear inequalities in two variables

Exercise 7.1 Graphing inequalities

1 (i) $x = -1, x = 5, y = -3, y = 1$

(ii) $x \geqslant -1, x \leqslant 5, y \geqslant -3, y \leqslant 1$

(iii) (c)

2 (i) $y = x + 2, \quad y = x - 2, \quad x + 3y = 2,$ $x + 3y = 22$

(ii) $y \leqslant x + 2, \quad y \geqslant x - 2, \quad x + 3y \geqslant 2,$ $x + 3y \leqslant 22$

(iii) (a)

3 (i) The shaded area is the feasible region.

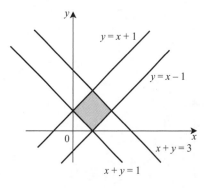

(ii) Square of side $\sqrt{2}$

(iii) Yes

4 (i)

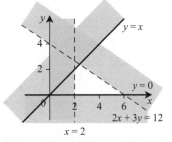

(ii) No

5 (i) $x \geq 0, \quad y \geq 0, \quad y < 2, \quad x + y < 4$

(ii) 7 points

6 (i)

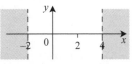

(ii)

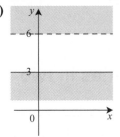

(iii)

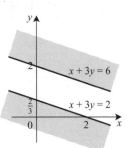

(iv)

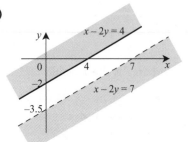

7 (i)

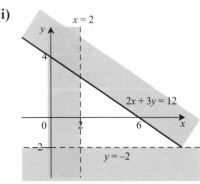

(ii) (a) Yes

(b) No

(c) No

8 (i)

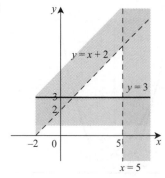

(ii) (2,3), (3,3), (4,3), (3,4), (4,4), (4,5)

(iii) The number of viable points increases from 6 to 15.

9 (i)

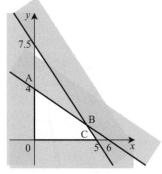

(ii) (0,0), (0,1), (0,2), (0,3), (0,4)
(1,0), (1,1), (1,2), (1,3)
(2,0), (2,1), (2,2),
(3,0), (3,1), (3,2)
(4,0), (4,1), (5,0)

(iii) Max value of $x + y$ is 5.4.

10 $I = 6.6$

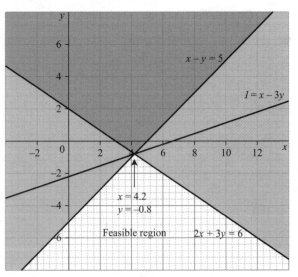

11 (i) $t = 0.06\,\text{s}$ or $3.94\,\text{s}$ (2 d.p.)

(ii) $3.88\,\text{s}$ (2 d.p.)

(iii) This is a 'show that' question, so a short answer cannot be given here. See the full worked solution online.

12 (i) (a)

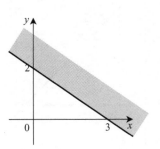

(b)

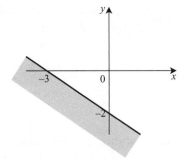

(c)

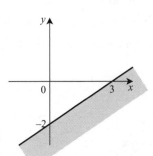

(d)

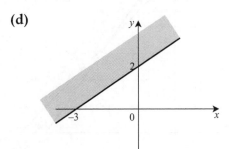

(ii)

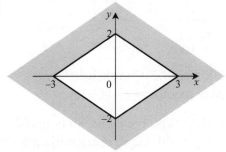

Rhombus.

13 (i)

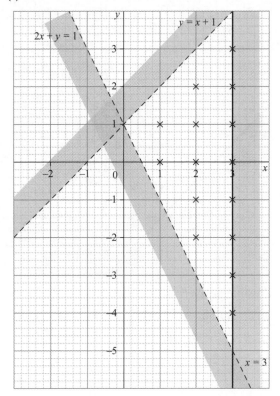

(ii) $(1,0), (1,1)$
$(2,-2), (2,-1), (2,0), (2,1), (2,2)$
$(3,-4), (3,-3), (3,-2), (3,-1), (3,0), (3,1),$
$(3,2), (3,3)$

14

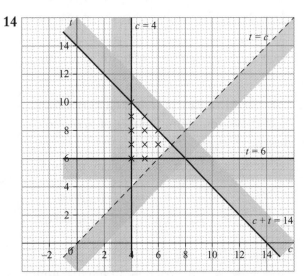

Possible answers:

$4c, 6t; \quad 4c, 7t; \quad 4c, 8t; \quad 4c, 9t; \quad 4c, 10t;$

$5c, 6t; \quad 5c, 7t; \quad 5c, 8t; \quad 5c, 9t;$

$6c, 7t; \quad 6c, 8t$

15 $c + d \geqslant 4$
$c + d < 8$
$c > d$
$d \geqslant 1$
$c \leqslant 5$

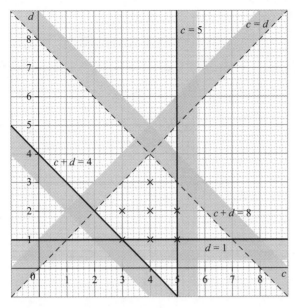

Possible answers:

$3c$, d; $3c$, $2d$;

$4c$, d; $4c$, $2d$; $4c$, $3d$;

$5c$, d; $5c$, $2d$

Exercise 7.2 Using inequalities for problem solving and linear programming

1 $x \geqslant 8$: at least 8 tables

$y \geqslant 16$: at least 16 chairs

$3x + 2y \leqslant 120$ number of hours of machine time

$8x + 3y \leqslant 240$ number of hours of assembly time

2 $x \geqslant 20$: Must have at least 20 luxury boxes.

$y \geqslant 0$: No minimum number of premium boxes.

$\dfrac{x}{25} + \dfrac{y}{17} \geqslant 1$ Restriction if all are premium boxes

$\dfrac{x}{42} + \dfrac{y}{50} \geqslant 1$ Restriction if all are luxury boxes

$\dfrac{x}{160} + \dfrac{y}{72} \leqslant 1$ Restriction on the maximum number of chocolates.

3 (i) $a \geqslant 0, c \geqslant 0, a + c \leqslant 500$

$c \geqslant \dfrac{500}{3} \Rightarrow c \geqslant 167$ (whole number)

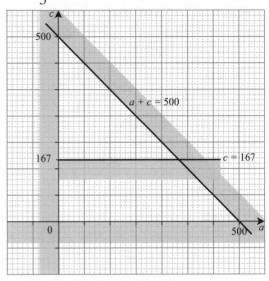

(ii) $P = 12a + 5c$

(iii) £4831

4 (i) $x =$ no. of prams, $y =$ no. of pushchairs

There are 4 wheels on each.

2000 wheels available $\Rightarrow x + y \leqslant 500$

1200 stickers available $\Rightarrow 3x + 2y \leqslant 1200$

(ii)

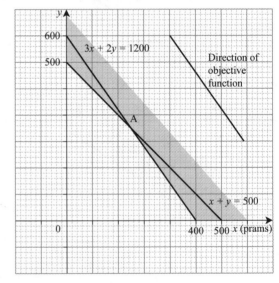

(iii) $C = 100x + 70y$

(iv) 200 prams, 300 pushchairs

Max income = £41 000

5 (i) $x + 2y \leqslant 80$ since max 80 hours labour.

$x + y \leqslant 60$ due to restriction on funds

(ii)

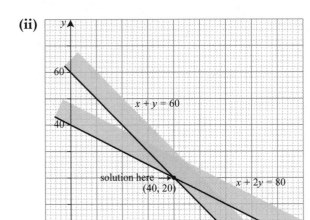

(iii) Profit $= 15x + 25y$

(iv) 40 of type A and 20 of type B
Profit $= £1100$

6 (i) $0 \leqslant s \leqslant 11; \quad 0 \leqslant f \leqslant 10; \quad f \leqslant s \leqslant \dfrac{4}{3}f$

(ii)

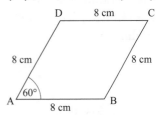

(iii) (a) $(11, 10)$

(b) $(11, 8\frac{1}{4})$

(c) $(10, 10)$

(d) $(8, 6)$

7 Best options are 7 large or 6 large and 2 small

8 Trigonometric functions

Exercise 8.1 Sine and cosine rules

1 (i) $x = 4.7\,\text{cm}$ (1 d.p.)

(ii) $x = 4.2\,\text{cm}$ (1 d.p.)

2 (i) $\theta = 52.9°$ (1 d.p.)

(ii) $\theta = 49.5°$ (1 d.p.)

3 (i) Area $= 8.9\,\text{cm}^2$ (1 d.p.)

(ii) Area $= 8.0\,\text{cm}$ (1 d.p.)

4 (i) $\theta = 36.9°$ (3 s.f.)

(ii) Third side $= 3\sqrt{5}\,\text{cm}$ ($= 6.71\,\text{cm}$)

5 (i)

C

8 cm

7 cm

80°

A   B

(ii) $B = 59.5°$ (3 s.f.)

(iii) $AB = 5.27\,\text{cm}$ (3 s.f.)

6

D   8 cm   C

8 cm   8 cm

60°

A   8 cm   B

Area $= 32\sqrt{3}\,\text{cm}^2$

7 (i)

D   C

4 cm

60°   6 cm

6 cm

A   B

$AD = BC = 2\sqrt{7}\,\text{cm}$

(ii) $AB = DC = 2\sqrt{19}\,\text{cm}$

8 (i) This is a 'show that' question, so a short answer cannot be given here. See the full worked solution online.

(ii) $c = 9.23\,\text{cm}$

9 $C = 72°$
$a = 3.09\,\text{cm}$ (3 s.f.)
$b = 6.98\,\text{cm}$ (3 s.f.)

10 (i) $PQ = 3\sqrt{5}$
$QR = 3\sqrt{5}$
$PR = 9\sqrt{2}$

(ii) $\hat{P} = 18.435°$
$\hat{Q} = 143.130°$
$\hat{R} = 18.435°$

(iii) This is a 'show that' question, so a short answer cannot be given here. See the full worked solution online.

Exercise 8.2 Trigonometrical identities

1 This is a 'prove that' question, so a short answer cannot be given here. See the full worked solution online.

2 (i) $\tan\theta = \dfrac{1}{2}$

(ii) $\theta = 26.6°$ or $-153.4°$

3 (i) $3\cos^2\theta - 2 = 0$

(ii) $\theta = 35.3°, 144.7°, 215.3°$ or $324.7°$

4 A is point $(63.4°, 0.9)$

5 (i) This is a 'show that' question, so a short answer cannot be given here. See the full worked solution online.

(ii) $1 - 2\sin^2 x$

6 (i) This is a 'show that' question, so a short answer cannot be given here. See the full worked solution online.

(ii) 5 and 3

7 $x = 120°$ or $240°$

8 $x = 54.7°, 125.3°, 234.7°$ or $305.3°$

9 This is a 'show that' question, so a short answer cannot be given here. See the full worked solution online.

10 This is a 'show that' question, so a short answer cannot be given here. See the full worked solution online.

9 Applications of trigonometry

Exercise 9.1 Applications of trigonometry in 2D

1 RS = 13.8 km (1 d.p.)

2 (i) $\angle ADB = 13°$

(ii) AD = 187.9 m (1 d.p.)

(iii) DC = 39.1 m (1 d.p.)

3 (i) 10.1 m (nearest 10 cm)

(ii) 25.0 m (nearest 10 cm)

(iii) 73.0 m^2 (1 d.p.)

4 (i) 036° (nearest degree)

(ii) Area = 4811 m^2 (nearest square m)

5 Distance from starting point = 2.624 km (nearest m)

6 Height of hill = 74 m (nearest m)

7 (i)

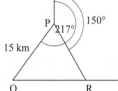

(ii) AB = 896 m (nearest m)

(iii) 853 m (nearest m)

8 (i) $\angle$LAB = 60°, $\angle$LBA = 70°

(ii) AB = 4.08 km (2 d.p.)

(iii) speed = 8.2 km/h (1 d.p.)

9 (i)

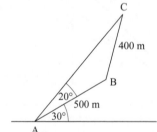

(ii) PR = 13.8 km (1 d.p.)

(iii) QR = 15.9 km

(iv) Speed = 61.9 km/h (1 d.p.)

10 (i)

(ii) $\angle$ACB = 25.3°

(iii) AC = 831 m (nearest m)

(iv) Gradient BC = 3.8 (1 d.p.)

Exercise 9.2 Applications of trigonometry in 3D

1 (i) 15 cm

(ii) 18.4° (1 d.p.)

(iii) 13 cm

(iv) 34.7° (1 d.p.)

2 (i) 3.2 cm (1 d.p.)

  (ii) 116 cm³ (3 s.f.)

  (iii) 480

3 (i) 61.9° (1 d.p.)

  (ii) 69.3° (1 d.p.)

4 (i) $10\sqrt{2}$ cm

  (ii) $15\sqrt{2}$ cm

  (iii) 20.31 cm (to 2 d.p.)

  (iv) 82.9° (1 d.p.)

5 (i) 26.6° (1 d.p.)

  (ii) 20 m³

  (iii) 5.1 m

6 (i) 25.9 m (1 d.p.)

  (ii) 297.0 m (1 d.p.)

7 (i) 38.7°

  (ii) 0.24 m³

  (iii) 0.11 m² (2 d.p.)

  (iv) sloping side = 32.0 cm
     Cost = £1.38

8 (i) 50.02 m (2 d.p.)

  (ii) 1.7° (1 d.p.)

  (iii) $6\frac{2}{3}$ m

  (iv) 7.2 m (1 d.p.)

  (v) 1 750 000 litres

9 (i) Least distance = 3.15 m
    Greatest distance = 3.73 m

  (ii) 14.8° ⩽ angle ⩽ 17.6° (1 d.p.)

10 (i) 914 m from A
    761 m from B

  (ii) 542 m (3 s.f.)

  (iii) 534 m (3 s.f)

10 Permutations and combinations

Exercise 10.1 Probability diagrams

1 $\frac{5}{12}$

2 (i) (a) 0.12

    (b) 0.4

    (c) 0.3

  (ii) 0.12
    $P(A \text{ and } B) = P(A) \times P(B)$

3 (i)

	1	2	3	4
1	2	3	4	5
2	3	4	5	6
3	4	5	6	7
4	5	6	7	8

  (ii) $\frac{1}{4}$

  (iii) 0

4 (i)

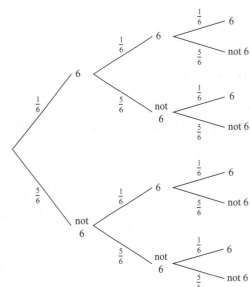

  (ii) $\frac{1}{216}$

  (iii) $\frac{2}{27}$

5 (i)

	Balcony	Box	Circle	Stalls	Total
Children	31	21	96	187	335
Adults	58	23	101	109	291
Total	89	44	197	296	626

  (ii) $\frac{22}{313}$

  (iii) $\frac{202}{7825}$

6 (i)

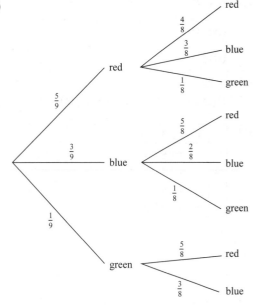

(ii) $\dfrac{2}{9}$

(iii) $\dfrac{3}{8}$

7 (i) A and C

(ii) 0.2

(iii) $P(A) \times P(B) = 0.15 \neq P(A \text{ and } B)$

8 (i)

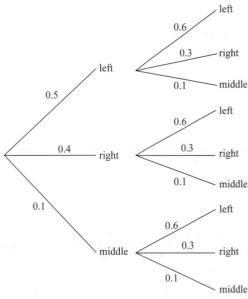

(ii) 0.57

(iii) $\dfrac{10}{19}$

9 (i) $\dfrac{2}{3}$

(ii) $\dfrac{41}{55}$

10 (i) 0.5

(ii) $\dfrac{5}{7}$

11 (i) $\dfrac{152}{315}$

(ii) $\dfrac{83}{304}$

12 (i) $xy = \dfrac{1}{3}$

(ii) $x + y - \dfrac{1}{3} = \dfrac{23}{28}$

(iii) $P(A) = \dfrac{7}{12}, \quad P(B) = \dfrac{4}{7}$

13 (i) $\dfrac{2}{15}$

(ii) $\dfrac{7}{15}$

(iii) $\dfrac{2}{15}$

Exercise 10.2 Permutations and combinations

1 120

2 36

3 $\dfrac{7!}{4!}$

4 1296

5 5040

6 462

7 $n = 9$

8 (i) 528

(ii) 3168

9 $\dfrac{49}{54}$

10 (i) 3003

(ii) 9

(iii) 714

11 (i) 362 880

(ii) 5040

(iii) 80 640

(iv) 282 240

12 $x = 7$

13 (i) 362 880

(ii) 80 640

11 The binomial distribution

Exercise 11.1 Binomial expansion

1 $y^4 - 12y^3 + 54y^2 - 108y + 81$

2 $32x^5 + 80x^4 + 80x^3 + 40x^2 + 10x + 1$

3 $1024 - 25600y + 288000y^2$

4 $4096w^{12} + 73728w^{11} + 608256w^{10}$

5 $1 - 8x + 28x^2 - 56x^3$

6 4032

7 -81648

8 10264320

9 (i) $a^3 + 3a^2b + 3ab^2 + b^3$

　(ii) $x^3 + 6x^2y + 12xy^2 + 8y^3$

　(iii) $1 + 3x + 6y + 3x^2 + 12xy + 12y^2 + x^3$
　　　$+ 6x^2y + 12xy^2 + 8y^3$

10 (i) $a = 3; b = 2; n = 10$

　(ii) 103680

Exercise 11.2 Binomial distribution

1 (i) 0.046656

　(ii) 0.186624

　(iii) 0.813376

　(iv) 0.23328

　(v) 0.76672

　(vi) 0

2 $\dfrac{625}{11664}$

3 0.187 (3 s.f.)

4 (i) $\dfrac{1792}{6561}$

　(ii) $\dfrac{2912}{6561}$

　(iii) $\dfrac{6544}{6561}$

5 $\dfrac{7}{64}$

6 (i) $\dfrac{5103}{16384}$

　(ii) $\dfrac{4547}{8192}$

7 (i) 0.00104 (3 s.f.)

　(ii) 0.0608 (3 s.f.)

8 (i) 0.263 (3 s.f.)

　(ii) 0.387 (3 s.f.)

9 0.1323

10 (i) X is the number of successes of an experiment which is repeated for a finite number of trials.

The outcome of each trial is either a success or failure.

The probability of success remains constant, and each trial is independent of all others.

　(ii) X = number of heads from ten tosses of a fair coin.

'Ten tosses' $\Rightarrow$ finite number of trials;

'Head' = success;

'Fair coin' $\Rightarrow$ probability = $\dfrac{1}{2}$;

A coin does not have a memory so the trials are independent.

12 Exponentials and logarithms

Exercise 12.1 Exponentials and logarithms

1 (i)

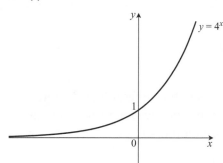

　(ii) $y = 0$

2 $x = 4$

3 16×8^x

4 $y = 2^x$ is graph D

　$y = 3^x$ is graph C

　$y = \left(\dfrac{1}{2}\right)^x$ is graph A

　$y = 2 \times 3^x$ is graph B

5 $y = x^5 - 2$

6 (i) $85°C$

　(ii) $42.7°C$ (3 s.f.)

7 (i) $\log_a (15xy)$

　(ii) $\log_2 (8x)$

　(iii) $\log_a (3w)$

8 $y = \log_3 (7x) + 4$

9 $x = 2.524$ (4 s.f.)

10 (i) This is a 'show that' question, so a short answer cannot be given here. See the full worked solution online.

(ii), (iii)

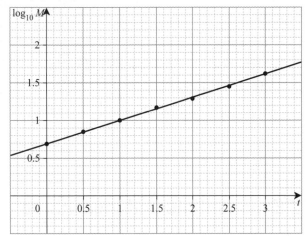

(iv) $a = 4.90$; $b = 2.04$

(v) 84.9 mg

11 (i) 60 kg

(ii) 49.587 kg

(iii) 8:16 pm

12 $x = 3$

13 (i) This is a 'show that' question, so a short answer cannot be given here. See the full worked solution online.

(ii), (iii), (iv)

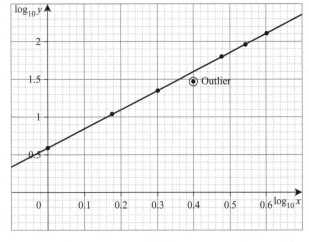

(v) $n = 2.45$; $k = 10^{0.60} = 4.00$
$y = 4.00x^{2.45}$

14 $x = 1.12$ (3 s.f.)

15 $x = 8$

13 Numerical methods

Exercise 13.1 Solutions of equations, including iteration

1 This is a 'proof' question, so a short answer cannot be given here. See the full worked solution online.

2 $x_1 = 2, x_2 = 0, x_3 = -1$

3 (i) This is a 'proof' question, so a short answer cannot be given here. See the full worked solution online.

(ii) $1.7 < x < 1.8$

4 $2\frac{1}{4}$

5 (i) This is a 'proof' question, so a short answer cannot be given here. See the full worked solution online.

(ii) $0.724 < x < 0.725$

(iii) $x = 0.72$ (2 d.p.)

6 (i) $x_1 = -2, x_2 = 4, x_3 = 1$

(ii) This is a 'proof' question, so a short answer cannot be given here. See the full worked solution online.

7 This is a 'proof' question, so a short answer cannot be given here. See the full worked solution online.

8 (i) $x = \sqrt[3]{2x - 3}$

(ii) $x = -1.89$

9 (i)

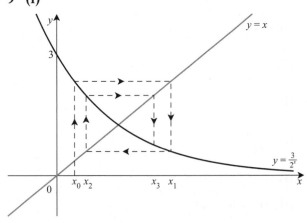

(ii) $x = 1.3$ (1 d.p.)

10 (i) e.g. $x_0 = 1 \Rightarrow \beta = 0.6527$ (4 d.p.)

(ii) α and γ

(iii)

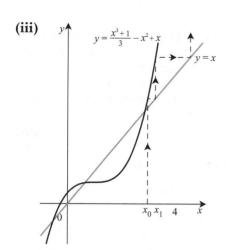

$$y = \frac{x^3+1}{3} - x^2 + x$$

$$y = x$$

Exercise 13.2 Gradients

1 3.3 (1 d.p.)

2 **(i)** 4.5

   (ii) 5

   (iii) 4.5 because it is the gradient between two points which are closer to (4,2).

3 **(i)** 0.0396 (3 s.f.)

   (ii) e.g. 0.0414 (3 s.f.)

   (iii) The point used is closer to (10,1).

4 **(i)** 0.5

   (ii) −2.5

   (iii) 3

   (iv) −3

5 **(i)** $2.7\,\mathrm{km\,h^{-1}}$

   (ii) $20.0\,\mathrm{km\,h^{-1}}$

6 **(i)** $4\,\mathrm{m\,s^{-1}}$

   (ii) $t = 4.32$ seconds

   (iii) $3.47\,\mathrm{m\,s^{-2}}$

Exercise 13.3 Areas

1 $3 \times 3 < A < 3 \times 5$
   $\Rightarrow 9 < A < 15$

2 15

3 **(i)** 4.216 (3 d.p.)

   (ii) Overestimate

4 Lower bound = 90
   Upper bound = 114

5 **(i)** 43.71 (2 d.p.)

   (ii) Use more trapezia.

6 12.49 (2 d.p.)

7 **(i)** 20.98

   (ii) 20.98 is the distance travelled in metres.

8 **(i)** 0.528, 1.194, 1.632, 1.960, 2.221

   (ii) 7.54 (2 d.p.)

   (iii) Overestimate

14 Differentiation

Exercise 14.1 Differentiation

1 **(i) (a)** $6x^2$

       (b) $12x^3$

       (c) $20x^4$

   (ii) (a) $4x + 1$

        (b) $9x^2 + 4x$

        (c) $16x^3 + 9x^2$

   (iii) (a) $x^2 + x$

         (b) $\frac{4x^3}{3} + x$

         (c) $2x^5 + 2x^3$

2 **(i) (a)** $2\pi r$

       (b) $4\pi r^2$

   (ii) $\dfrac{\mathrm{d}V}{\mathrm{d}r} = 2r\dfrac{dA}{dr}$

3 **(i)** $4x + 5$

   (ii) $3x^2 - 2x + 1$

   (iii) $32x + 8$

4 $k = 2$

5 **(i)** $3x^2 - 2x + 2$

   (ii) 18

6 **(i)** $3x^2 - 12x + 2$

   (ii) −7

   (iii) $y = -7x + 19$

   (iv) $x - 7y + 83 = 0$

7 **(i)** $9 - 3x^2$

   (ii) 6

   (iii) $y = 6x - 2$

   (iv) $x + 6y + 49 = 0$

8 **(i)** $3x^2 - 6x$

   (ii) 0

   (iii) $y = -5$

   (iv) $x = 0$

9 (i) $y = 9x - 16$

(ii) This is a 'verify' question, so a short answer cannot be given here. See the full worked solution online.

(iii) -52

10 (i) $2x + y - 15 = 0$

(ii) $x - 2y = 0$

(iii) This is a 'verify' question, so a short answer cannot be given here. See the full worked solution online.

11 (i) $3x^2 - 10x + 6$

(ii) When $x = 0$, $\dfrac{dy}{dx} = 6$

When $x = 2$, $\dfrac{dy}{dx} = -2$

When $x = 3$, $\dfrac{dy}{dx} = 3$

12 (i) $y = x - 7$

(ii) $(-2, -9)$

13 (i) $y = 11x - 33$

(ii) $x = -\dfrac{5}{3}$

14 (i) $3x^2 + 6x - 7$

(ii) P$(1, -7)$ and Q$(-3, 17)$

(iii) $y = 2x - 9$ and $y = 2x + 23$

(iv) 256 sq units

(v) Trapezium

Exercise 14.2 Stationary points

1 (i) $\dfrac{dy}{dx} = 3x^2 - 12x$

$x = 0$ or $x = 4$

(ii) max when $x = 0$, min when $x = 4$

(iii) $x = 0 \Rightarrow y = 4$ (max)
$x = 4 \Rightarrow y = -28$ (min)

(iv)

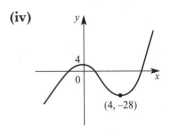

2 (i) $\dfrac{dy}{dx} = 4x^3 - 16x$

$x = -2$, $x = 0$ or $x = 2$

(ii) min when $x = -2$, max when $x = 0$, min when $x = 2$

(iii) $x = -2 \Rightarrow y = 0$ (min)
$x = 0 \Rightarrow y = 16$ (max)
$x = 2 \Rightarrow y = 0$ (min)

(iv)

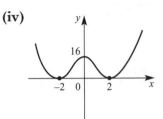

3 (i) $\dfrac{dy}{dx} = 9 + 6x - 3x^2$

$x = -1$ or $x = 3$

(ii) min when $x = -1$, max when $x = 3$

(iii) $x = 3 \Rightarrow y = 27$ (max)
$x = -1 \Rightarrow y = -5$ (min)

(iv)

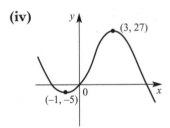

4 (i) $\dfrac{dy}{dx} = 4x^3 - 12x^2$

$x = 0$ or $x = 3$

(ii) Point of inflection when $x = 0$, min when $x = 3$

(iii) $x = 0 \Rightarrow y = 6$ (pt of infl)
$x = 3 \Rightarrow y = -21$ (min)

(iv)

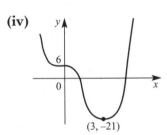

5 (i) (a) $\dfrac{dy}{dx} = 2x - 3$

$x = 1.5$

(b) $\dfrac{dy}{dx} = 3x^2 - 6x + 2$

$x = 0.42$ or 1.58

(ii) (a) min at $(1.5, -0.25)$

(b) max at $(0.42, 0.38)$, min at $(1.58, -0.38)$ (all to 2 d.p.)

(iii)

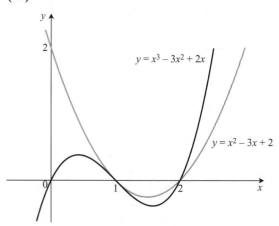

6 (i) max $\left(-\frac{2}{3}, 4\frac{13}{27}\right)$, min $(2, -5)$

(ii)

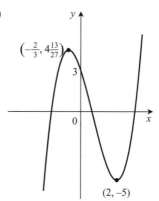

7 (i) $a + b = -2$

$2a + b = -7$

$a = -5, \ b = 3$

(ii) This is a 'show that' question, so a short answer cannot be given here. See the full worked solution online.

8 max $(-2, 11)$, min $\left(\frac{2}{3}, 1\frac{14}{27}\right)$

9 (i) $p = -9, q = 10$

(ii) max $(-1, 15)$, min $(3, -17)$

(iii)

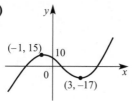

10 (i) max $(-1, 6)$, min $(1, 2)$

(ii)

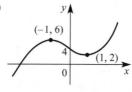

(iii) Increasing for $x < -1$ and $x > 1$

(iv) Decreasing for $-1 < x < 1$

11 (i) $b = 3a - a^4$

(ii) $3a^3 - 3 = 0$

(iii) $a = 1, \ b = 2$

(iv) This is a 'proof' question, so a short answer cannot be given here. See the full worked solution online.

12 (i) $a - 8b + 16c = 20; a = 4$

(ii) $12b - 32c = 0$

(iii) $a = 4, b = -8, c = -3$

(iv)

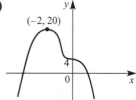

13 Stationary point is $x = 1$; Max volume $= 18 \ \text{cm}^3$

The rest of this question is a proof question, so a short answer cannot be given here. See the full worked solution online.

15 Integration

Exercise 15.1 Introduction to integration

1 (i) $y = 2x^2 - 2x + c$

(ii) $y = x^3 + x^2 - x + c$

(iii) $y = 5x + c$

2 (i) $f(x) = \frac{x^4}{4} - x^3 + x + c$

(ii) $f(x) = \frac{x^3}{3} - 2x^2 + 4x + c$

(iii) $f(x) = 4x - x^2 + c$

(iv) $f(x) = 4x + c$

3 (i) $x^3 + c$

(ii) $x^3 + x^2 + c$

(iii) $x^3 + x^2 + x + c$

(iv) $3x + c$

4 (i) (a) $y = x^2 + 2$

(b) $y = x^2 - 1$

(c) $y = x^2 - 4$

(ii)

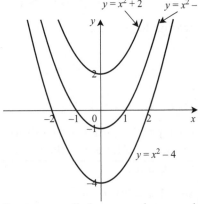

Curves are all the same shape and size but displaced vertically.

5 (i) (a) $y = x^2 - 8$

   (b) $y = x^2 - 1$

   (c) $y = x^2 - 8$

(ii)

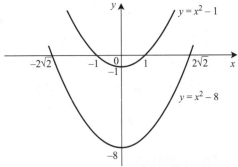

Curves are all the same shape and size but displaced vertically. **(a)** and **(c)** define the same curve.

6 (i) $\frac{2}{3}x^3 - \frac{x^2}{2} - x + c$

(ii) $\frac{4}{3}x^3 + 2x^2 + x + c$

(iii) $\frac{x^4}{2} - x^3 + x + c$

7 (i) $y = \frac{2x^3}{3} + 4x - 6\frac{1}{3}$

(ii) $y = \frac{x^3}{3} + x + 16$

(iii) $f(x) = \frac{x^3}{3} + x^2 + x - 5\frac{2}{3}$

(iv) $f(x) = \frac{x^3}{3} - x - 4$

8 (i) $y = 2x^2 - 3x + c$

(ii) $y = 2x^2 - 3x$

9 (i) $f(x) = x^3 - 3x^2 - 4x - 2$

(ii) $(4, -2)$, $(0, -2)$ and $(-1, -2)$

10 (i) $x \pm 1$

$(x = -1$ is maximum, $x = +1$ is minimum$)$

(ii) $y = 2x^3 - 6x + 3$

(iii)

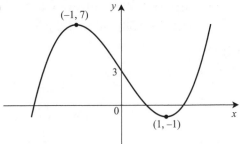

11 (i) $y = x^3 - x^2 - x + 1$

(ii) $\left(-\frac{1}{3}, 1\frac{5}{27}\right)$ and $(1, 0)$

(iii)

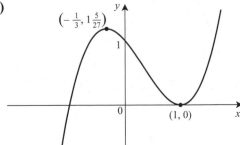

12 (i) $\frac{dy}{dx} = x^2 - 2x$

$= x(x - 2)$

$= 0$ when $x = 0$ or $x = 2$

$\Rightarrow \frac{dy}{dx} = x^2 - 2x$ is a possible gradient function.

(ii) $\frac{dy}{dx} = c(x^2 - 2x), c \neq 0$

(iii) $y = \frac{x^3}{3} - x^2 + 2$

Exercise 15.2 Definite integrals and areas

1 (i) $2\frac{1}{3}$

   (ii) 33

   (iii) 24

2 (i) 8

   (ii) 18

   (iii) 42

   (iv) 36

   (v) $-1\frac{1}{3}$

   (vi) 0

3   **(i)** $4\frac{2}{3}$ units^2

    (ii) $3\frac{3}{4}$ units^2

    (iii) $\frac{4}{27}$ units^2

    (iv) $2\frac{2}{3}$ units^2

4 $10\frac{2}{3}$ units^2

5   **(i)**   Area A = 4 square units
           Area B = 4 square units

    (ii) 0

    (iii) Areas above and below the x-axis have cancelled out.

6   **(i)**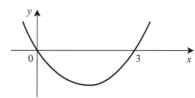

    (ii) $0 < x < 3$

    (iii) 4.5 units^2

7   **(i)**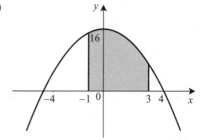

    (ii) $54\frac{2}{3}$ units^2

8   **(i)**   A(−1, 1), B(7, 17)

    (ii) $85\frac{1}{3}$ units^2

9   **(i)** $y = -4x + 8$

    (ii) $2\frac{2}{3}$ units^2

10 (i) $x + y = 1$

    (ii) 4800 cm^2

11 (i) $3\frac{5}{6}$ units^2

    (ii) $408\frac{1}{3}$ m^3

16 Applications to kinematics

Exercise 16.1 Motion with constant acceleration

1   **(i)** $v = u + at$

    (ii) $v^2 = u^2 + 2as$

    (iii) $s = ut + \frac{1}{2}at^2$

    (iv) $s = \left(\frac{u+v}{2}\right)t$

2   **(i)** $s = 5$

    (ii) $t = 12\frac{1}{2}$

    (iii) $a = 2$

    (iv) $v = -3$
           Travelling in the opposite direction to the initial motion.

    (v) $u = -3.5$
           Set off in the opposite direction to the final motion.

3   **(i)**   time = 1.28 s

    (ii) speed = 12.5 m s^{-1}

4   time = 2.45 s

5   acceleration = 1.25 m s^{-2}

6   **(i)** $a = 1.25$ m s^{-2}

    (ii) $s = 162.5$ m

7   **(i)** $v = 40$ m s^{-1}

    (ii) Total height = 181.6 m

    (iii) Total time = 15.17 s

8   **(i)** $t = 1.6$ s

    (ii) $s = 6.4$ m

    (iii) After 3.2 s

    (iv) After 0.2 s and 3 s

9   **(i)** $t = 2.5$ s

    (ii) $s = 6.25$ m

    (iii) $v = 2.5$ m s^{-1}

10 (i) $33\frac{1}{3}$ m s^{-1}

    (ii) $a = 1\frac{1}{3}$ m s^{-2}

    (iii) $\frac{5}{24}$

11 (i) After 2 seconds

   (ii) For stone 1, $v = -5\,\text{m}\,\text{s}^{-1}$

   For stone 2, $v = 5\,\text{m}\,\text{s}^{-1}$

Exercise 16.2 Motion with variable acceleration

1 (i) $v = 20$

   (ii) $a = 12$

   (iii) $a = 24$

2 (i) $s = t^2 + 3t + 2$

   (ii) $s = 2$

3 (i) $a = 4 - 6t$

   (ii) $s = 2t^2 - t^3$

   (iii) $t = 2$

4 (i) $v = 6t + 3t^2$

   (ii) $s = 3t^2 + t^3 + 6$

   (iii) $t = 2$

   (iv) $s = 26$

5 (i) $t = 2$ or $t = 3$

   (ii) $t = 2, a = 1\,\text{m}\,\text{s}^{-2}; t = 3, a = -1\,\text{m}\,\text{s}^{-2}$

   (iii) $v = \dfrac{1}{4}\,\text{m}\,\text{s}^{-1}$

   (iv)

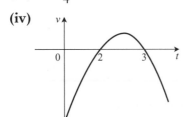

6 (i) $v = 14 - 9.8t$

   (ii) $t = 1\dfrac{3}{7}\,\text{s}$

   (iii) Max height $11\,\text{m}$

   (iv) $a = -9.8\,\text{m}\,\text{s}^{-2}$

   Acceleration due to gravity.

   Negative since ball ascending.

7 (i) $a = c_1 + 2c_2 t$

   (ii) $c_1 + 4c_2 = 6$

   (iii) $x = \dfrac{c_1 t^2}{2} + \dfrac{c_2 t^3}{3}$

(iv) $2c_1 + \dfrac{8}{3}c_2$

(v) $v = \dfrac{9}{4}t^2 - 3t$

8 (i) $12\,\text{m}$

   (ii) $12\,\text{s}$

   (iii) $v = 6\,\text{m}\,\text{s}^{-1}$

   (iv) This is a 'show that' question, so a short answer cannot be given here. See the full worked solution online.

9 (i) After $20\,\text{s}$

   (ii) $a = 1\,\text{m}\,\text{s}^{-2}$

   (iii) $s = \dfrac{t^2}{2} - \dfrac{t^3}{60}$

   (iv) $s = 66\dfrac{2}{3}\,\text{m}$

   (v)

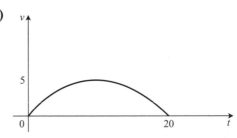

   Distance = area below v–t graph

10 (i) $v = 8\,\text{mm}\,\text{s}^{-1}$

   (ii) $t = 4\,\text{s}$

   (iii) It changes direction.

   (iv) Max $v = 9\,\text{mm}\,\text{s}^{-1}$

   (v) (a) $26\dfrac{2}{3}\,\text{mm}$

   (b) $30\,\text{mm}$

11 (i) $x = 4\,\text{m}$

   (ii) $v = 8 + 2t - 3t^2\,\text{m}\,\text{s}^{-1}$

   (iii) $a = 2 - 6t\,\text{m}\,\text{s}^{-2}$

   (iv) Max $v = 8\dfrac{1}{3}\,\text{m}\,\text{s}^{-1}$

   (v) $t = 2$

   $x = 16$

   (vi) Distance $= 12\,\text{m}$

12 (i) $a = 3t^2 - 8t + 4$

   (ii) $t = \dfrac{2}{3}\,\text{s}$ and $t = 2\,\text{s}$

   The particle is slowing down.

   (iii) $s = 8.25\,\text{m}$